Both Boys Climb Trees They Can't Climb Down

Both Boys Climb Trees They Can't Climb Down

Stephanie Yorke

Clarise Foster, Editor

EDITIONS

Cover design by Doowah Design.
Photo of Stephanie Yorke by Johanna Matthews.

This book was printed on Ancient Forest Friendly paper.
Printed and bound in Canada by Hignell Book Printing.

We acknowledge the support of The Canada Council for the Arts and the Manitoba Arts Council for our publishing program.

Library and Archives Canada Cataloguing in Publication

Yorke, Stephanie, 1985-
    Both boys climb trees they can't climb down / Stephanie Yorke.

Poems.
ISBN 978-1-897109-94-6

    I. Title.

PS8647.O573B67 2012   C811'.6   C2012-901742-6

Signature Editions
P.O. Box 206, RPO Corydon, Winnipeg, Manitoba, R3M 3S7
www.signature-editions.com

To my grandfather, Terence Sanford
(despite the coarse language)

Contents

Variations on a Cardboard Crown

Brothers

I've known Absalom with his wrists
bent over the frets;

I've known Solomon with one foot
on the staircase.

I've known Absalom to waste
entire Saturdays wrapped in bed, watching his aquarium —
when the fish turn, his ribs flicker.

I've known Solomon to press his face against
oak banisters, and plan
to eat tiger in Africa,
shoot rubies in Sheeba

with the queen on her throne like the lump in his throat
when he teaches her two mantras:
breasts like pomegranates / chasing the wind.

And Absalom sets his sobs between his sister's,
their hair wet, and lungs
nosing the surface;

now he's after the man with a knife,
gripping, and flying off, the handle.

I've known Solomon to clasp
the knees of foreign gods,
and adorn his prayers with floor plans:
love me back / cites I'll build.

Here's Absalom, sleeping in a pup tent,
signing war statutes he hasn't read.

Here's Solomon cutting his heart and initials
into the bark of Lebanon's cedars.

Both boys climb trees they can't climb down —
neither's calling for a ladder.

Cities I'll Build

Prophets Helping Prophets

I.

Mo

mo-mo-cess

Moses smells
like a bitter old
shrove, chronically unleavened
on his hitched tongue.

In compensation, he received
a wooden stick.
Pardon. Staff.

He had a whip back in Egypt.
Harder every time
he stuttered.

Especially those camels.
Chewing when they should pull.

Israel. You chomping mule.
If that whip weren't a sea behind —

II.

Tiresias

wears a blindfold.
Just so folks know
to step around

when they meet him in frescoes
and tragic plays.

He also carries a seer-stick,
tapping Athens to Thebes
with his forecast

while the king packs
picnic lunch. Clarity waits

outside the polis with his staff,
playing x's and o's in the sand pit.

He needs that second sight
to know who won.

III.

So

Moses and Tiresias
hooked up one Saturday,
eating lamb satays
and laughing about drought.

Then, these tablets —
said Mo.
It was like having jugs.

Tiresias laughed.
Wait till I tell you —
women would smash theirs, too,
if they could.

snicker groan Hera   oh figs
mutter Aaron cough Canaan
HA Thebes oh Thebes Dionysius.

Then, lifting a skewer, screwing
cubed meat with desert lips,

Tiresias asked,
Do you still have teeth?

No, me neither.

Is it the naked gums
that they won't listen to?

said one prophet; the other nodded.

Co-evolution

Crows are bored. Hucksters with meal tickets.
Mobsters with tax exemptions.

They pick on garbage bags because garbage bags are stupid,
and because crows are racist,

all Roman nose, battalions grown fat
on pax cul-de-sac.

Crows chased the glint in running brooks.
Until sardine cans.

This crow pokes a half sardine, asking him
to please swim away please.

Then, I will chase you!
Next time you see a crow,

say something stimulating.
Offer him a crossword puzzle.

Dr. Asimou

Sorry. Turns out the machine is growing
less and less human. Personal computers
gladly repeat what they just said, let you choose
the wallpaper. Dump trucks carry their load
till there's a good time to unload,
and signal their intentions with orange
warning lights. The dashboard GPS
continually asks pertinent questions,
and cell phones can be turned off at the theatre,
whereas your friends. Even simple radios
just tell you; cut and dry, or unplugged.

But, the umbrella! Push a button, he's open,
squeeze a shoulder, he's shut.
When it rains, I say, I, Robot.

Creation

In the beginning, God got school supplies:
pencil crayons, loose-leaf, a pink eraser.
And, because he was finally in grade four,
a math set. His mother thought he'd lose it,
so she picked a cheap one, rickety-hinged
tin box painted to look brass, protractor
out six degrees, and every metal gadget
preemptively rusted.

God felt noticed.
Danny's set had a stainless steel ruler;
Kenneth's was in a smart wooden case.
That's the one God smashed over his desk;
Mrs. Void sent him to sit in the hall.

On the way out, he snuck his drafting compass
into his breast pocket. Outside, on the cool tile floor,
he drew a circle, Alps and Himalayas
wherever the pencil slipped. He made
semicircles called day, night, water, dry earth,
then etched little figures inside —
algae, ferns, ostrich, horses, bipeds —
man, God was on a roll!

Mrs. Void forgot him completely.
Late on the sixth night, as God yawned,
his school janitor happened by,
whistling with his broom:
What you done, son?

God showed him creation.

Now, boy-all — isn't that some good?

Captain Hook's Gator

Well the hand was so good —
sauce in the knuckles, cracking
like forty-cent wing night.

I've followed him ever since.
Over wound clock in my stomach, counting
Hook-love, Hook-love —

Hook's a star.
Perm. Accoutrements. Platforms.

I'm his fan base: can't disentangle
my appetite for him, from my appetite for him.

i.e.: I love to see him in tabloids,
but would I want it to be true?
Hook pregnant? Caught Cheating? Anorexic? Swallowed whole?

Been licking my chops for the rest.
Licking stamps for my fan mail,
white perforated teeth.

Cautions

Yellow signs say caution, wet floor —
depict death-by-footstep,

walking with his jacket open,
the dog off-leash.

Yogurt-white barking
teeth — syringes cocked.

The vaccine risky, disease incurable.
Wing-tipped avian flu.

A feather duvet, and police in the doorway
ask questions about the attack:

Well officer, supper looked like Loch Ness.
Broken wishbone on my soup spoon;

pin digs trachea ribs,
this injunction called swallowing.

Undercooked meat; birth complications; premature kittens.
Respect the incubation period.

Don't forget the oven! In case of fire,
never go back for the cat.

Clogged flues, curtain piled on the register —
an eyelid out of place.

Pompeii

You wake thirsty.
Your parents have left
and taken the beach umbrella.
They've sectioned off your television room
with a velvet rope.

Your housesitter cuts the rope
with a paring knife.
The velour is easy to snip, but
she grits and oaths over the hidden chain,
a spine beneath the skin of an eel

or trout, the first food you notice.
The TV trays are laden, readied.
Pull-aparts, almond compote
(nuts like drugged eyes)
and shrimp with pricked capillaries,
white and pink as a child's purse.
Emmm.
Leg of muscular duck.

Tipping sauces on the carpet,
you binge with the housesitter.
Then divine the feast back out, feather
jollied through the first valve of your throat.
Make way make way

for the second course: You swallow swallows,
their birdseed eyes unlit.
A wild cherry between peppery birds.
Seeds and twits.

The volcano spits like a roast pig,
initial ash on your window.

To Her Husband, With His Nose in the Latest *Frommers*

Imagine how in heaven we'll be double platinum
tourists in a cloud-coloured bus with 'Promised Sight

Seeing' across the side in pearl and gilt, above the tagline
'The Bus with MANY Bathrooms!' Ether air brakes

huff and heave past defunct Russian satellites, rocket husks,
Saturn's ice and Jupiter's backlit moons

with their burnished explanatory placards:
'this stone laid by the Prime Mover

to commemorate and delight our elect retirees'
in stud headphones and anti-nausea bracelets, swigging ichor

-pink gravol, reclining and napping in gastrically induced
air-conditioned bliss. An angel

-stewardess with bleach-blonde wings and cheeks
pink as the gravol

offers sanctified louse-free mini pillows
and lite tonic water and low-gluten rice snaps

to the lion and lamb cuddled over a high gloss
issue of *Cosmo*, humming the bridal march. Brings back memories,

Darling. You gave me the window seat, so now
you lean across with your long-barrelled camera,

clicking, anticipating our eternal home
full of snap frames and adhesive photo corners.

I don't mention that your flash reflecting
in the pink-tinted window will ruin every shot;

I don't mention your lens cap, your finger on the viewfinder,
my nose in the last frame. Why correct you,

when our guaranteed satisfaction hasn't stopped in millennia.
Or the mink-white stewardess. Or the bus.

But we'll see what develops when you send that film
to the finishers' dank basement.

Busts

Sotto voce. White halls with artificial
air circulation remind you of the shower

stall without water. Halves of men,
circa two through nineteen hundred,

in victors' garb, a mangy animal skin
tied at the shoulder, a toga,

an armoured vest or militant breast pockets,
marble laurels, a spear-tipped crown.

Some with eyes blanched — philosophic. Refrigerator light.
Some with caverns in place of eyes

or pupils, fixed straight or off left
where they've just glimpsed winged victory

and a crow raiding the garbage.
We've made these men

with the exacerbated frontal lobes, foot-long jawline,
flat ears, piqued ears, furrows and smooth

-unto-womanhood lips, latinesque noses and ostogoth shoulders,
and perhaps the whole rock head

scaled up by half. With perfunctionary hair,
or the meringue hair of trained

musicians, opened collars and yanked cravats.
If these show a little bare chest

under the voice box's dented protuberance
and the clavicle's thumb-sized carport,

it must be bare chest — our foremost sculptor
never accomplished rough curls

more convincing than pubic hair
fastened into a cake of soap.

The Oracle at Truro

Near express checkout four,
a bin of MULTICAT kitten-farm-caliber
cat litter

rose,
levitated,
like a pelvically-nested swami
ascending on the steady elevator of his proverbs.

A discreet miracle.
So I poked the woman ahead of me,
who carried a baby with muffin cap ears.
The lady flinched, turned away,
and smashed the interac keypad
as if she were phoning a prized and furious lover;
I hope their quarrel ended in french toast.

Still the litter rose, like the soul of a dead balloon.
Bashfully slow.

The other checkout standers
smelt of chloroform. We
were dilapidated teens and amnesia-stricken men and
unimaginative mothers with misaligned hips.

Why all this litter?
Some for cats, cat families.
Some for icy driveways.
Some for sopping must-smell in wet basements —

Oh! The saturated human eyes!
Liquid paper faces. We sweat.
Can none of us open our jackets?

And on each arm, MULTICAT litter,
and in each cart, MULTICAT litter,
a special-purchase-maximum of five bins,
though one had transcended.

Telephone Lover turned to the cashier,
pummelling my face with her baby.
But the blow was eased by the coiled pastry of his ears.
No tears. And the child's brain was forked.

He pulled a scroll from the ass of his snugglebyes,
steered the paper to my hand.
I unscrolled:

    In the year that the Elm trees died,

I would have read on,
but the checkout girl was asking for my cards.

I fumbled them like amateur tarot.

Pup Tent

The Flamingos

Bill, let us go to the zoo.

In the swamp tank,
the hippos are snout-to-snout,
warm fat noses and lips.
Delicate and bubbled up,
whispering stories.

The polar bears sleep closely,
bellies and paws.
Though it's July.
If one had a popsicle,
I am sure he would spilt it in two.

Crackerjack? Aw thanks Bill, I'd love
some. But Bill?
I can't reach from here.

The single monkey beats his chest.
His bottom is bright.

But then again, there are the flamingos.
Their knees bending backward and so weakly.

Roman Candle

-A roman candle is a cheap firecracker.

1.

What do you do with the roman candle
after the older boy hands it off,
chasing its harried fuse;
that boy you've eaten worms for, bought popsicles,
pelted with gravel, love;
when he hands it off and says, Quick, in the mailbox,
a Halloween greeting, engorged with itch, converting
static and ash-tipped to here and pow.

2.

Here and pow — tomorrow's an excuse.
But a fuse! Like a tongue engorged with spice
as heat bleats through your eye-walls and bullied rear throat,
rime of curry powder on your soft palate.
It's your peppercorn; cough or swallow.
Hold or throw. It's all in your hands —
this separate and colossal thumb fostering
off its rough pulse.
Half zipper tooth, half boot tread,
quick low heat, staccato and roughshod.

3.

Unlike children, a fuse
works toward something.

4.

Everything you ever heard in church:
Hide it under a bush? Oh no!
I'm gonna let it shine.

So you plant the roman candle
in Nancy McCann's mailbox, hinges inquiring,
then smacked for their petulance.

Run to the boy. Braced,
ears covered, but eyes opened wide —

      — Of course my eyes are open!
      I don't want mere evidence,
      glory's peeled sardine can.
      No see-my-hands-my-side tripe.
      I want the blood in front of me.

He's a keeper.

5.

Now, mid duck-and-cover, you'll recollect
that visit; her wooden spoon violence and powder keg breasts.
Aunt Rita in the trailer, waits on Jack
and readies the air for her verbal embolism; tongue swelling
with vitriol, toxic potential, she'll show him what, tell him where;
her dishrag and thick wrists, twisting;
a blast she'll deliver, radiant and clear
as the slide in your View-Master
held up to the light.

Pull the red lever; what comes next?

6.

Jack comes home dry,
along with the roman candle.

There stays the neighbourhood,
manicured trees.

Uncover your ears.
Will he even look over?

Rita (and Jack's), Tomato Season

Bring beers for Rita; red and breasted
like a bear cub's un-depleted wet nurse;
bring dark-necked beers
for this rough-necked queen,
big as Greenland,
red as a nosebleed on Nordic snow.

A flake in her snow globe, Jack
shifts utensils in the drawer.

He and Rita together
lick the platter clean,
but Rita licks it first.

In an apron broad as a mainsail
stirring, she brews big
Christmas carol-cheeked tomatoes
into ketchup, vinegar
a loud flat note
in the First Noel.

To Rita I bow.
And consent to eat till I fissure.
And Jack's plate is gory,
a shield after the fight.

Rita, Ketchup, and Beer
hunker round a campfire,
compare knuckles and knives.

Ryan's House

Ryan bit kids at recess.
Clam-smiles on our arms.
His father was a banker, and wanted Ryan to learn chess,
and study hard with his *Hooked on Phonics* kit.
His mother had teeth like stacked toilet paper.
Ryan bit kids at recess. Wouldn't talk to the teacher —
not even when she took attendance. Present. Present. Present.
His mother sold Avon products with Avon catalogues
and lured other mothers to parties with free soap.
His father liked to indulge in oysters,
twin-pronged fork plucking each tongue.
And read aloud from the very difficult newspaper,
cause Hookt on Fonix really werkt for him.
Ryan hardly talked. But bit kids.
His older sister enunciated and tugged her shirt and stood on one foot
longer than anybody could.
One time the soap was shaped like a swan.
His sister had a sleepover for every girl on our street,
and Ryan was pacific till breakfast, when
he shut himself upstairs and stomped
above our heads; don't mind him, the father said, and flipped
the pancakes as only a banker flips pancakes,
and checked the spreadsheet of his wife's teeth.
The sister waited with her mouth shut.
The pancakes came out puffy and round but not cooked
in the middle — but we passed the syrup,
and listened to the house chew.

Delilah

Even when we ask point blank,
what was Delilah, Ms. Downie won't answer

prostitute and local hero; Delilah was a harlot,
wielding scissors on our Sunday School papers

over Samson's ram's back and battered curls,
face down in her lap, and his ass just covered

in animal fur like Downie's in archaism. Harlot.
Delilah fully dressed, even her head

dressed, sandals tied, a shepardess costume
undermined by drop earrings, unsavoury lipstick.

On the opposite page, Samson with his eyes all carved.
Short hair writhing and a tenable shake

in his loin cloth, one arm on each white pillar,
pushing out the supports. The stadium roof,

Ms. Downie explains. After the king
backhoed Samson's eyes, saw him jailed and chain-ganged,

and invited his thousand friends
to watch the tigers eat. Chalk-white sockets

turned toward the sky's blackboard, Samson
brings the roof down over their heads —

breaking them, she emphasizes.

Protest

You'd stopped, so I was trying to play —
e minor, a minor, none of us twenty,
and so hard to reach the frets —

evening lolled. I chewed my hemp
necklace, plaited fimo and glass.
Then your frayed cigarette,
before the others smoked.

Those guys were all home-rolled, politicized
to the tips of their hair, their sandals in socks,
leather ribs over wool guts.

The bongo drummer was beat,
and our signs had fallen from their posts:

TROOPS OUT NOW!
turned up at the sky.

We all share a moon.
This dark dinner hour,
preparing to rain.

Police watched the steam on your coffee.
You tested the temperature, then the taste —
a flux of breath in the covered cup.
Another fumbled chord.

Coronet Player

you've got tang like a thin blue devil
and hair like a crown of thorns

you fine trashed mutt,
nursed on sticky rice and Saint Hubert.
I think of anime on birthday napkins
deli-section sushi geisha and Minolta

amplified —
your sweet-devil shoe on
the black-water stage
your bombs-away tie square
as tae-kwon-do at the neck.

A row of manicured buttons,
your fingernails
braid: horn, throat, ear.
The song is crowned.

You are a novel spice,
or a graft of bamboo.
Mason jar, water and stone.

Public Works (After Hours)

Drunk, he told it like it wasn't. Dumbly,
piecemeal, just fine — verbosity's nothing
beyond his sweet voice deep as truckloaded
gravel the boys dump and spread with shovels.
He glances sideways, like a tired foreman
pinches up a cigarette's quick secret —
just hope he'll flick the ash off and tell you
some of the saltier details, like brine
soaked olives that knock your taste buds straight off.

Good. Taste has never been the tongue's real work.
It's best as a trowel striking the gruff root
of the tree you might plant tomorrow;
near a crude house on a bald lawn.

At the Matinee

The shutz of a velcro nursing bra —
a film with an archer and a lost unicorn.
Kim's kids with pupils blown big as dimes
wishing well; shadows on the reel,
trash in the water.

In the hitch between frames, Kim hears
foyer hum, the ticket man's minimum wage jokes,
the popcorn machine and its hurt tom-tom.

Baby gloms on the vast, gum-worn breast.
Hobble-hinged seats with their pilled upholstery,
Kim's third child, gymnast of the flip-back chair
(the one, they chime, that doesn't know its father)
Mom, what do unicorns eat?

Sweetie I'm not sure. These Saturday kids
with piqued interest and fizz in their drinks.
Some toddle in the aisle, stick pennies in their mouths.
Others run eyes like a tongue over every
enchantment, choking hazard.

The archer threads his bow, sights a cream flank.
In the foyer, boys plain as the one that held her
hum a vegas-me-three-cherry-wish-karaoke,
push the wide brooms.
Cinema uniforms, mutable chests.

The archer has a crisis of the heart, relinquishes.
Kim's half-glad; she's seen worse films.

The popcorn machine with its hurt
tom-tom trying one dud seed,

clack and bake in the metal drum.
A narrow pupil, fixed in an eye;
one burnt kernel in the popcorn machine.

Rebound

Don't go home with that one.
She's got a name tattooed on the bottom of her foot;

she doesn't want to be lifted.
She wants to list her aches and cramps,

tear an ear when she menstruates,
or call it a migraine, shot nerves.

She sucks twice on a thermometer,
sings a low song in the shower,

hates you for asking, won't tell you
what it was. But you know you heard

her foot against the no-slip mat, water
sluiced out through the arch —

the long way she calls out.

St. Margaret's Square

Crowned with swingsets, inlaid with a pool.
Every third day, you wiggle into
your puddle shoes, and ride the bus
with a bag of sandwich crusts.

The delight of your old age
(since the death of your responsible spouse)
has been eating

to the perimeter of honey and jam
and no further, saving that
for the fowl.

Crusts float like cork.
The ducks, with their trowel beaks,
dig in ferociously,
wringing food through their throats.

But the swan,
pipette-necked,

is choking at the moment.
Your crust fits like a tampon.

Her spit glands buckle. Also her wings.
Black, her feet rake the water,
as a tickled child might kick.

Her neck is an S, then a cold I,
long and bristling.

You pass the bread bag, fist to fist.

On the swingsets, the assembled crows
caw, caw.

Morning, 1921

After "Morning" by Lawren Harris

Clothesline in a slump; or, call it a crescent,
sheets hung double and a single blue towel,
one boy in the family. 1921:
something roaring somewhere else,
house not lipstick, but barn red,
knuckle pink where the sun hits
broad planks, brush strokes, crude joints,
twin back doors separated by a drainpipe
that rends in the cold as he dreams of buckling bobskates,
wakes, sets down his feet:
the floor frosted. The bedroom windows
peek out through the roof, flawed
glass in the gap between pale curtains, overlooking
the back fence, a broken slat where the cat escaped,
two broken where the dog followed,
and drug-out bootprints where the boy ran after,
into long-shadowed night. Now the dog and boy
are up with his mother, quiet in the kitchen. The kettle
warms, but will not boil.
She sets her hand against it, and the other against her stomach,
waiting for a kick. And the roof
thaws a little, collects
melt wherever the wood bows.

Houses, Richmond Street

After "Houses, Richmond Street" by Lawren Harris

Fewer shutters match, each time you visit —
some blue paired with orange, some green, some off
having their own experience.
But the windows retain their sills, and the sills are kept clean,
and every April women climb flimsy ladders
to rag and harangue mildew from awnings
over the doors. Every June the street sweeper
wishes the sidewalk back to white. Concrete
six inches thick, rather than meagre asphalt,
so the surface will never crumble (though
of course it's begun a little at the edge).

You choose your own house out from the row —
that house that hangs back from the road, always
the last swimmer into the pool,
toes drawn up. You walk toward it, past
the same forked tree– but now the fork is higher,
so boys can't reach to climb. And men don't bother.

Sobs Between His Sister's

Parents

My father scraped a cat off the road.
Newly married; their first cat.
Later he'd rub kitten noses in shit

when they'd gone behind the TV set,
both daughters howling animal rights. He was
the flea bather; the pill inserter;

the shoveler. But Mom
microwaved a saucer of milk
to feed each nose-christened kit,

her palm between the poor little
shoulders, after his stern thumb.
She couldn't even turn on

a vacuum, till she'd raised
the alert: mime-cleaning
with the detachable brush

while tail-tips vanished under the couch.
Ears flat to the roar. And the sound of my father's
car in the driveway —

the ancient cough when it stopped,
the double scrape of his boots
in the entry. Six green eyes

fierce as a tire tread, up from behind
my mother's blue jeans —
but her look, gone glad and soft.

Observe the Lilies of the Field Arrayed

Mercury so low, it plumbed her care.
Boy in his unders before the wood stove:
she pushed his head through a flannelette
shirt neck, bowl cut sent to feather.
Socks, then leggings: a hand on her neck
for balance, gravity-ticked shin.
Another of socks, and a corduroy
overall, stern metal clip at each shoulder.

A balaclava (glad moment, robbing banks) on nose,
cheeks, forehead, a scarf over the nose again,
socks. Toes as buried money: unlike Matthew's
householder, she'd be satisfied with the same coins.
She worked his feet through elephantine
ski pants, tightened the snow bib
over the sneak down the small of his back.
Then, she taught him the secret: gloves
under knit mittens, then the waterproof sort.

Open hand or blunted fist, he reached for the jacket
on the seat of the three-legged chair.
No, she told him; that'll be the finishing touch.

Developmental Stages

I'd begun to pull her earrings, so she let
the holes grow over — just pulled the fishhooks
from the lobes, dropped them on her bureau.
Thought, now I'm a cold fish. She razed her hair
off in a cap, when I'd learned to chase
the sheen on that hair, learned to make a fist.

She left off the summer sandals, the covered toe
tapered to a difficult, white point —
he'd once bragged, you're light as air. She grasped
the bath ledge, slouched under water.

She'd jingle the car keys, laugh at my laugh.
I remember she wore sweatpants and a slack polo shirt.
Her vaccination scar peeked out of the sleeve,
a coin in a shallow pond:
brighter once it's thrown.

Mother

The jellyfish catches
granules of everything.

She is a freelance lymph node,
a naked allergic eye.

Ever light a candle blindfolded?
How quietly she extends.

But it stings her each time
a wave doubles back.

Her scrim flesh bevels,
accumulating noise.

Bird Feeding, February

My mother fed the birds
by proxy. With her rheumatoid, only Dad could carry
ten kilos of mixed seed
from the Co-op, his chapped grip
on the paper-plastic weave
as the jays ganged to call.

He took the bag over his shoulder,
knifed open the thatch over
my kiddie slide's three-step platform,
parapet of our flat neighbourhood.
Mum with her silty coffee
and sandbagged immune system, watched

small birds nickel and dime
through each inch span
while the grosbeaks got
like cash in hand. Robins
begun more and more to overwinter, drew
worms in the mistaken thaw.

My mother cheated too: methotrexate. Binoculars
out the kitchen window, that extra
zoom. The amused way she had
of watching their want. The way
satiation channel surfs
desire — the limp way we watch

television sports, players who still
have it in them to rise and go
whistle-sure. Grosbeaks smashed
sunflower kernels. Fine birds

worked beady nijer seed
while I, on the floor, shook

all my crayons from the box.
Mom's crinkled fingers around the binoculars
(a hand full of party streamers,
she sometimes said) and one hooked
through her mug, a customer bonus
with the Pfizer logo come off in chips,
pecked in the dishwasher.

Parade

Fresh surgeon's tread where they'd tried the elbow, again —
we were late for the check-up, traffic jammed
by the Provincial Ex Parade.
HANDS said the smock on the first 4-H-er,
      and the other H's came behind
as your toe wandered between null brake and null gas.
Next the petting zoo, goat champ and tug
      in the back of a half-ton,
kittens and rabbits in arm, jesus as calm —
      halved laudanum tablets.
Then the Feeds n' Needs float and Farmer's Dairy,
      touch and go flatbeds,
melancholic suspension. Stewiacke Senior Brass following
a round man with a further drum strapped to his stomach,
mallets like a robot wearing mitts.
His many wives on horn, puffed permanent rippled hair
      and baby blue cadet hats,
diabetic veins throbbed through their nylons,
      seams of ore just under the earth.
Shock in all the ankles as they stomped out
4/4 time.

You watched the heat gauge touch zero.
The representative from Carnival Day Amusements
      stalked behind a Xerox banner,
      BRACELET DAY TUES
breasts a mortal threat to her shirt and I'm sure
stretch marks inked to mint green snakes.
Finally, the singers dressed as rodeo stars, fake spurs,
Hank and Dolly, a pinch of tired under the eyes.
You told me you disapproved of country music —
mourning stories.

Young mother. Every night you watched two repo men
shoulder your cleanly detached legs, slam the van doors, and go.
You woke knowing surreality was the leak in your basement,
staunched it with a faded towel, flicked on the perk.
Said loud to my door, Honey, it's pushing seven,
          better get the papers out.

After the parade, you slid the key in the ignition
like an anonymous threat into a letterbox.
The clot of cars was just as slow; but held to gain.

Steve Urkle on TGIF

Dad worked Friday nights, so rather than family
dinner we got to hunker in the den,

television and us three bent goat-wise
over the cookie sheet she'd baked

the fries and fish sticks on. I traced
each crinkle in each cut fry

with hands full around the plastic ketchup bottle.
Calligraphy, paint can — Fridays no Dad

asked, blah blah blah learn at school today? Soundtrack
applause as the dork in red glasses

burst onto the set, greeted Carl the usual way.
Mom said, I don't know how he speaks

through his nose like that. She told me to stop,
when I tried to imitate.

Riding the Elephant

Dad's wallet and his head shook as one. I watched
the attendant sort coins into her tray; I climbed
raw wood steps to the platform, where grown hands
boosted me into the metal frame.

A howdah? No kidding around. I wasn't
Infanta or Queen of the Raj — I was a sales-flyer-class
birth-order-victim, vying against my baby sister
for ice cream bars and bop-em gator tokens,
for tickets from the long blue strip
Mom kept furled around her hand,
tight under the thumb.

It only takes two for the haunted house —

No. These have to last till we get home.

I shared my elephant with two others:
a young man who always faced the sun,
drying his pimples; another with his shirt collar
poorly smoothed after the wash. Men must be kept
apart, so I was stuck in the middle —
slouched between them like a sodden tea bag,
brother's old shorts down past my knee,
hair stretched hard against my greasy scalp,
wandering partition between two braids.

The elephant's spine rolled like a hurt snake
as he started to walk.
                              Some elephant.
I might have been riding an office worker,
a typist coaxing the pain through his neck
as the attendant hauled on the tongue harness —

no whip crack, no questions asked. I wished
for the elephant to lift his nose,

but the pendulum was slack. Now fresh
round footprints eclipsed old footprints; now my father
exchanged his head for a camera
pointing up, turning to jog a few steps,
again pointing up, saying my name like a new name.
Smile. I heard the lens motor, as Camera Man
took a long stride back.

You look so small up there.

The grey back like a knuckle, giant
felled last week; feet heavy as hushed
adult conversation, and a furrowed brow
that consumed the whole face.
Except the eye: a pool of strong coffee.
Eyelashes thick as a mug handle,
eyelids I could arm wrestle, and lose —
but the wetted sawdust would not stir,
so he had no reason to blink.

Verses for a Late Middle-Aged Potter

1.

His pottery wheel
repeats that word until it's solid;
ear protection keeps his thoughts separate
from the motor's psychic channelling, its aggregate
pitch. The way everything speaking is nothing
speaking, the soprano natter
in spaces between vertebrae
convening in the concert shell of his lower back,
as corrugated thumbs draw the cup sides up, and out:
teach the thrum to stay
put.

2.

His pottery wheel
repeats that word, but won't pronounce it —
gives advice with ball bearings in its cheek
as re-toothed old men
say retirement, say recession
at a mumble that wears down the brain, fills the head
with the importance of setting
attentions, like cup sides, up, and out —
look ahead. But the potter looks down,
labours in the clay's wrinkled weight,
knotty as a crumpled ear, taught to stand
as an O
-pen mouth.

3.

His pottery wheel
had better learn the name; had better speak
up, to compensate the sky
for the depth of his concentration, his hours spent
watching thumbs tip the clay edge
up, and out; the sun's hours
spent watching the glint of his baldness, his eyes
wet as the clay, wet with it, not tracing
the horizon but training
a new one,
one that curves.

4.

What we talk around, but never utter — talk
constant as a zipper
that avoids-saying till it climbs its own teeth. Talk
constant as the children, for years
chiming for help with their winter coats —
da-de, da-de — a decade
of their arms wide, marking
the gulch of ability,
a mitten on either bank. He doesn't need
these confetti-pieced demands, to know
every jacket must be shut to the chin,
and every pantry crock
needs a lid
that fits.

5.

His pottery wheel
repeats that word, and moves under it — a would-word
churned in four hundred watts
he spliced from the car battery
with a couple jumper cable clips —
my father's found his own outlets.
He dabs his fingers, and adapts
his trimming awl to the wobble in the wheel, his eyes
downward, fixing the vessel
with a curled clay lip
that can hold without measuring — that can teach
our perishables to settle
on earth.

Before the School Play

What are aunts for. The curling iron
plugged in beside the toaster.
So she could pretty my bangs, afterward.

Braid at the turn in my skull —
comforts whispered, at that turn
might catch the weave, lock in memory.

But she only spoke of the work. Some
glad you've not showered today,
a little grease keeps it together.

(In that kitchen, grease the great enabler.)
We'll mail a video to your da.
His stocky girl in a denim one-piece

with pearlette buttons, lace
collar. Some lines I had to read
highlighted on a page,

pieced shadow where the photocopier —
Aunt's pulling forced my eyes
onto the ceiling light. Green splotches

pulsed and slid — my own
blood on its tour of duty.
Each round, a setup for the next.

Chicken Guy Din

Low, blunt bangs — her waiting eyes
a dipper just above the pool;
a latent moon, low on the horizon. Cast over
her schoolbook, coffee, window, coffee —
the window settles it. Facing down an empty driveway.

Dad pulls in. It's a strain to hear the gravel
spit above the family sheltie yodelling,
blue paw pads on the window's wooden lip.
Damn dog carries his tail straight, even when he's chasing it.

Toenails snapping, the clock chases its tail,
short-legged on the tacky kitchen floor.
The girl scoops up her worksheet and calculator
as Dad fights his key ring, then the lock.
Wrestling with one hand. So supper's takeout.

The bags crinkle. But listen closer. To the moon.
Hear it sigh, and say it's not the one full of holes,
and from where it sits, the earth looks like cheese.
An aged cheese, a green-pitted gorgonzola
stinking up the vast fridge of the universe.

How was your day? Dad crinkles.
Red dragons on the bags; would they ever breathe fire?
No, not if they're smart dragons.
Prints on paper. Good,

good, she says, then Good again, resealing her guy din.
She recycles her tins and juice cans,
but never finishes her meals.
So the only dirty dishes are forks and knives
in the unstopped sink.

She Emerges

Grandmother offers no advice. Instead,
she farts and apologizes, farts and apologizes,
covers her mouth so we'll think it was coughing.
Throat long as a camel's, old mule slippers,
she shuffles to the mailbox, circles each room,
little shakings lost in the thick, thick carpet.

The bear that follows her leaves no tracks.
She remembers the days of holding
cats in the bathtub, sinews and flea soap.
At the grocery store, she emerges shocked —
Cost of margarine! Cost of birdseed! *Cos —*
the terrible puff of the automatic doors.

Woman, I'm sorry. Your bread half-buttered,
raisin knees bared, house dress like a house plant,
a dark green aloe with darker green stripes. Venetian blinds
down so long, they've left slats on your eyesight.
Sundays on the telephone, you alternately claim,
it's an uphill battle, or, all downhill from here.
Would you warn me, if it were flat?

Grandmother Said

There's mouse traps in the basement, Girlie, some set —
so don't go down. There's wax-sealed
Cheez Whiz bottles of grape jam, and emptied Certo envelopes
piled on the defunct wood-burning stove, with its pig-nosed bolts and soot
thick as snow on the chest of the drunk who
found his coma in the drift, Sweet Girl,
there's an aloe plant, all curled octopus fingers
calling you close. There's a mounted jigsaw
of the Taj Mahal with the Raj guard standing out front, at attention, atop
the student-sized pump organ from Kit's estate:
it's got no buttons, and what buttons there are
lost their felt, and what felt there is
wasn't green to begin with, sure as Christ's side, all the ivory's gone
and the soft and forte pedals fallen like bad arches
that'd get you out of Vietnam. There's a draft down there. There's a bent
hockey stick, a trapper's mitt and dried Ontario peach pits
we saved on the dream of fledging a tree —
like hell it'd take this cold soil — we used to winter up here,
so we've got seventy-five back issues of the Reader's Digest,
including that old special on the lunar landing.
But they're not in order. They're bookended
by a chipmunk-shaped peanut butter canister
filled with pennies too rank to count, copper gone blue and sour
like a mouldering graveyard full of Queen Elizabeths. There's a rotted
sewing basket, a purple ski-doo jacket,
an empty ant farm, unhatched sea monkeys, an airforce
plaque with a brass albatross,
and a dynamo lamp, broken. The old dog's dish, the old dog's collar,
the dog's red ball with his bite still in it, smiling. Resting under
that autographed print of Expo '67, and on the wood-panelled frame,
our complete collection of the animals from Red Rose tea.
There's the HAM radio headset beside the crushed banana boxes
saved for kindling when we replace the stove — plus we broke

a bottle down there last week, might be slivers —
just you stay away from those steps, Miss.
C'mon — I've got a lemon pie in the fridge.

Extended Family

Suppose we are passing the salad, eyes on the tongs
clawing one cherry tomato —
then hand the bowl off to Aunt, and Uncle
says Whoa wifey! When did you take to the greenery?
Pinching her left arm.

We avert everything,
even the utensil sound,

except my twenty-year-old avatar, who shells
out her fluid tongue and diagnoses his antagonistic
machoist promontory tendency.
Rah-rah university
pastiche.

Then Seventeen steps in loud
flowered flip-flops chucks a waterglass and shouts Fucking raw!
Why not just stab her with your fork, Dumbfuck? Or get a divorce.
I'll never get married, or at least not to —

Writ on infinite scroll. Enter mute
Fourteen in her giant verdict
-still-out-on-this-breast-thing shirt, pity
for her aunt melding with pity for herself, and in self
pity, saying nothing. Good thing prelapsarian Ten

stomps in wicked awesome bicycle helm
-et and delivers her bottom lip like
a hammerhead sizing up a nail —
yet the slow-jawed family chews leaves,
brave as beefcattle,

as Seven rises in narcissist oblivion,
gap teeth announcing I would have won the science fair, 'cept
my volcano broke.

Three is bull red and confused at this
gathering, talk. Snorting
she takes her purple heart sweater and sinks
her incisors into Uncle's palm. Finally

Mother's excuse to holler, Don't! Stop that!
as we evaporate with relief.

Variations
on a Cardboard Crown

In Memoriam 1979-1997

BFF (I still have the string necklace)

1. Highway 102 Shoulder, Spring, 1993

I've got you tonight, in your Burger King Crown
out under the highway — the semis hauling
axels overhead. We climbed the embankment,
down off the road, so we wouldn't get caught
with our sleeves rolled, the click of small fires. We pass
fumes back and forth, feel the thrill in culverts
as water bucks its cut path underground.

Your thumb on the ridged wheel — chip hard wrist bone.
Weather-beat, precocious. World-weary fourteen.
So when you turn to give the sudden maglite
the finger, you're no brat blurting a catch-all.
Knuckly finger, knows what-all it cursed.

The officer opens his notepad before he speaks.
Ladies. What seems to be the problem here?

2. Demographic

The Iliad, Abridged: today in class
they gave us each a page, word shadows
bent in the photocopied spine.

I was made to read first —
sounded *a-chill-ease* when I saw Achilles,
and the mistake carried through the whole class.

Sometimes, for want of medicine, one drowns the cat.
Our cosmetic treatments over junior high sinks —
you force hair sprigs behind your ears
while I douse the puff in my bangs.
Just stay down. We press, splash and fingercomb,
leave the faucets on.

At three, the tape-recorded school buzzer
shrieks like a buzzard coming, and we go
past the one-lane mall and the fast food strip.
All of our best memories, in these restaurants —

A mother's hand knocked
french fries from the carton to the tray,
notched the ketchup packets.

A father in shirtsleeves
reached at the drive thru; pulled paper foil
from one edge of your cheeseburger.
Honey, slow down. You'll burn your face.

Tonight, after a mall loll, we eat in
under lamps like a starship tractor beam,
nine slabs of backlit menuboard.
Look. The possibilities are endless.

3. The Baby-Sitters Club

That morning, you'd emptied your closet shelf.
Threw down the rattling hairdryer, and the book
series she'd subscribed you to by mail.
Her ash flaked off, and the books kept coming,
'big hugs' on the invoice.

Your bureau covered with Happy Meal toys —
all of our best memories are in restaurants.
The watermelon that's also a wind-up car;
the two-thirds downscaled Rubik's cube.

Forget that stupid jewellery box she left,
motorized ballerina. Gears claw through
'Over the Rainbow,' ready to seize.

Forget that bracelet she left in the box —
set in silver polish, the whole thing dissolved.
Not to tarnish her reputation.

.

In the days when we made owls from paper bags,
your mummy said, *alright Missy, you too.*
Sat me on the kitchen table, cut my bangs.
Christ, that was easy.

You looked at the floor:
a puddle full of earthworms, curled and straight.

.

She'd tried not to give you a trailer park name.
Bernadette. *There's three more in my row,*
you say, thumb pressed on your breastbone.
Someday I'm gonna be a doctor, ha ha.
Me with the wooden stick in your throat.
Jesus Fucking Christ. God's trailer park name.

4. Tetris

After breakfast, when you were playing a round,
your father put his foot on the kitchen trash,
taught you the other way to make things fit.

You know, I had a dream where you take that out.

Well I had a dream where you take that out.
Last time you broke the bag doing that.

Ceiling light there twice in his eyeglasses;
screen light on your face, fastened to the cheeks.

•

Angry crown jostled all over your head.
I'd like to beat him to a pulp, sometimes.
You don't even take pulp in your orange juice,
harsh silt in your throat, behind your eyes.

Your ponytail fuzzing apart at the sides
where you tried to pull a few strands down
for ringlets at the temple, like that tennis player.
Your thumbprints raw from the volley of shapes.

5. Ladies, what seems to be the problem here?

Your schoolbag marked in liquid eraser,
the A in its circle, the lopsided stars.
Your socks worn thin at the ankle bones,
each an outsized stone in a mood ring, a cheapie
that wouldn't change colour washed in tears.
Jawline sure as split wood — nutcracker arms
just a lever to make the teeth work.

I don't care who smoked first.
If she jumped off a bridge, would you do it too?

The draught of air
you find in the bottom of your pop cup.
Slurp and slurp echo — edge of the takings,
stop and start sound of Coke in your straw.
You smack the waxen butt against the table,
caramel brown pop drips caught in the ice.
Suck and tug at air. Eyes blown
big with will; sarcasm; the gasp.

6. Mars Observer, 1992

That winter, boots tall as an astronaut's.
You make new steps in plow piles, cut open
the footpath back to Steve's house.

Bald too early with his hurt look.
He says, *never trust anyone who's had an epiphany.*
You agree. Don't want miracle of the loaves
talk. Just enough bread, laid out.

He's the sort of guy who gets down to business —
to your white Kmart bra, the one shoulder strap
biting in, small breast hauled out of place.
The other strap slack: he slides it off,
doesn't stop to put his toes over yours,
crooked and cold as the snowbank you kicked
in your white Kmart boots — the moon
looks good, but who knows how thin it's sliced?
Your underwear waistband rolled on itself
three times, so it won't show over your jeans.
He unrolls the band, up past your navel,
looks at your eyes like incorrect change.
Sorry. You say. *Nan bought them for me.*

Scraping home in boots with insoles worn
down to the rougher plastic.

You set your feet inside your first boot prints,
but steps back aren't the same shape.

7. Highway 102 Shoulder, Spring

Dark so early? You wonder. You sniff
the inside of your wrist, almost the palm,
decide it isn't such a good perfume.
I am the heroine dealer's wife. Smell me.
Take the crown off, to re-centre the gems —
you're not married, and he doesn't sell drugs.
But pre-fab stories hotwire the tongue.
The father and lover should have fought.
Crown's 'ruby' scored in white. Read 'twinkling.'

The maglite-moon. False advertising.
The cop who'd *let it go this once*
while sparse stars rattled with big talk.
The sky a meagreness, spread far.

We breathed it again, and spent half an hour
chucking stones at a crushed pop can,
a glint in every dent. Damage winked and scraped,

like fork and knife in the next room.
Metal pricks, as your dad spears macaroni.
You sit with yours in front of the TV,
grab at the lever for the reclining chair.
Light of the sitcom on your chin, flickering
when the audience laughs.

What are you staring at?
We threw stones till the can skittered off.
We skittered off, made the joke twice.

8. 2001

A slide is changing: I am twenty-one
being asked to go to a long buffet,
candles under warming trays, wet cheese,
fastened name tags. For networking purposes.
Alright, Boss. I'll be sure to try the fish.

Those last nights, you watched me play Nintendo,
my small self stomping mushrooms with both feet.
Da — da — da — da-da-da-da-da—
You hummed the soundtrack a little too slow,
turned me down when I offered the controller.
Didn't like the other way to make things fit.

Your room is here ma'am, they've already started.
I cross the path of the slide projector,
duck under the harsh ray.

9. Prognosis

No, it's not like that — no chunks or anything.
Just loose in there, like ink in water.

He shut the passenger door. *Alright, Princess.*

Boys laughed. *Stevie's got himself a real snow queen.*

The women said, *with a figure like that,*
got to wonder where she keeps the liver.
Said, *she eats like she's got a hollow leg.*

That's not the gap.

You wake like you've been dumped from a sack.

Clothes hangers rattle and rake the bared post.

10. Highway 102 Shoulder, Spring

I've got you tonight, in your Burger King Crown,
hair out like the spray of a fireman's hose;
hair out like the spray of a burst hydrant,
crown set on the jaunt, a man with a cane
leaning forward, finger curled, calling me
close — *c'mere, I got something to tell ya* —

You're in the arc of a long story
about *did you see this guy in our class
just sat there pulling a thread on his socks,
so he gets up after, they're all frayed to shit*

you just sat there with your pencil gone blunt,
eraser worn down to the metal cusp —
when you take a word out, you leave grey scabs
or rip through to the next page.

There should be a robe flared out behind you,
ruby red with Dalmatian fur trim

read 'ruby'

so he stands up barefoot, and the teacher says

Notes

Absalom was one of King David's sons, as was Solomon. Stories about both characters are in the Talmud, the Qur'an, and II Samuel of the Old Testament.

Tiresias was a prophet who usually brought bad news. He features in many Greek tragedies, including Oedipus the King. His warnings were usually wilfully misinterpreted or ignored. He had spent part of his life as a woman, as a punishment for having offended Hera.

Lawren Harris was a Canadian painter, part of the Group of Seven. The paintings that these two poems grow from are his paintings of houses.

Steve Urkle was a character in the sitcom *Family Matters*.

'Observe the Lilies of the Field Arrayed' draws on a line from the New Testament.

For 'Variations on a Cardboard Crown':

BFF: Best Friends Forever. Very popular inscription on plastic/hemp/ nickel jewellery.

'The A in its circle': the anarchy symbol.

The Baby-Sitters Club: an extremely popular chapter book serial for girls, which came into publication in 1986.

Burger King Crown: a cardboard crown which Burger King Restaurants distributed during the early 1990's. The crowns were often worn as an ironic accessory by adolescents.

'I am the heroine dealer's wife, smell me': a sidelong reference to Michael Ondaatje's famous love poem, which was published in the late 1980's.

The Iliad, Abridged: Homer's famous poem, with the meter and some of the grittier plot details removed. A school text.

Kmart: a bargain department store chain, which was still prominent in Canada during the early 1990's.

Maglite: a brand of flashlight, which is often associated with the sort of spotlight-flashlight police use.

The Mars Observer: an unmanned Mars mission. NASA lost contact with the observer in 1993.

Semi: slang for a large transport truck.

'That Tennis Player:' the narrator cannot remember Steffi Graf's name.

Tetris: a video/computer game.

'The two-thirds downscaled Rubik's cube': the 2x2 'Pocket Cube' is much easier to solve than the traditional 3x3 model.

Acknowledgements

Poems in this collection have appeared in PRISM *International, The Fiddlehead, Grain Magazine, The Malahat Review, Descant, Bodies of Work, Encompassing Seas,* and other publications. "Bird Feeding, February" was short-listed for PRISM's poetry contest, and "She Emerges" was a finalist for the *Malahat's* Open Season Awards. "Rita (and Jack's) Tomato Season" was on the long list for the *Best Canadian Poems in English* annual anthology. An earlier version of "Delilah" was a finalist in Arc Magazine's poem of the year contest.

I'd like to thank mentors who've helped with some of this writing directly, including Ross Leckie, Patricia Young, Don McKay, Lynn Davies, and others. I'd also like to thank those who've nudged certain books my way, including Demetres Tryphonopoulos, Diana Austin, and John Ball. Thanks to Len Falkenstein for bringing really excellent plays to the stage in Fredericton. Thanks to peers who've had a say about some of the poems in this collection, including John Barger, Pat Leech, Danny Jacobs, Jennifer Houle, Carson Butts, and others. Thanks to my book editor, Clarise Foster.

I'd like to thank Leo McKay, for encouraging me early on.

I'd like to thank my childhood Sunday School teachers. Although their instruction may not have had the intended result, I am immeasurably grateful for their contributions to my imaginative development.

Finally, I would like to thank my wonderful family, and would like to note that the families and parental characters featured in the poems are creations of my imagination. This is not a work of autobiography.

Rave Reviews

"We all know that 'abundance' is not simply about money. Yet money is important in everyone's life, and this is a wonderful book for anyone who is facing a money challenge, or who simply wishes to create greater financial security. A fabulous mixture of spiritual tools and practical ideas for increasing money flow now. Highly recommended!" **Neale Donald Walsch, Bestselling author,** *Conversations with God*

"Sandy will accelerate your thinking and your bank accounts. I like her and her inspiring and insightful money magnetizing book." **Mark Victor Hansen, Co-creator #1 New York Times best selling series** *Chicken soup for the Soul®.* **Co-author,** *The One Minute Millionaire*

"If you want a book that will change your financial destiny forever - THIS IS IT! This is a compelling read that offers readers the philosophy and practical tools to begin creating and experiencing prosperity in a rapid time frame. I loved this book and the tools within it have transformed my financial reality time and time again. Being wildly wealthy is a choice and Sandy has showed me the HOW - and HOW easy it really can be for anyone." **Melissa Scott, Extreme Breakthru Coach, www.equinoxlifecoaching.com**

"How To Be Wildly Wealthy FAST, is a roadmap to financial success and abundance. The absolute best book on wealth creation I've ever read." **Jim Donovan, USA, Author -** *Handbook to a Happier Life*

"Your book is BRILLIANT. Your book has changed my life. I am happy, excited, inspired, and alive; and the blessing is that life is now returning blessings to me. As I said, your book is BRILLIANT." **Carole J Toms ND, USA**

"Your book is AWESOME! Extremely informative yet easy to read and even easier to apply. Since starting your book, my life has changed SO much! Everything came about SO fast for me." **Tracii Summers, Sydney, Australia**

"Your book is my very favourite book - and I've read quite a few self development books in my time! I am *so* grateful for this unique, incredibly powerful info." **Beverley Rilatt-Richardson, Australia**

"I received your book and I read it super fast because I love it! I am over-joyed with abundance and prosperity and very good things are happening to me now! Thank you." **Gabriella Baglia, USA**

"I have read many books related to this subject but this one has to be the top of my list" **Amanda, New Zealand**

"Sandy, you are walking, talking, living proof of the power your book contains. You've put the most important secrets people need to speed up the process for increased wealth! You're doing a fantastic service to the world." **Jason Oman, USA, #1 Best-selling co-author of** *Conversations with Millionaires*

Success Stories

"I used one of your techniques and was surprised when a cheque arrived in the mail for some work I did a long time ago. I was expecting maybe $100 to $200; I received $3300." **Chris, Australia**

The first day after I completed one of your strategies I received a check for $2121 (I had expected around $800). Less than two days later I received $15,000. Then less than two day after that, I received another $10,000. This absolutely works." **Christine W. USA**

"I just had an increase at work – it was supposed to be $5,000 but ended up being $15,000!!!" – **Amanda, Australia**

"Business is increasing and I received a tax cheque of $9000 when I expected to break even with my taxes – I was thrilled!" **Amanda, Melbourne, Aust.**

"I have a large network marketing organization and it has dramatically increased. Thankyou, Thankyou, Thankyou!" **Jean M.S. Brisbane, Aust.**

"Two weeks after reading the book a friend gave $1000 (no strings attached) and I received a further $100 from an anonymous friend!" **Jan W, NSW, Aust.**

"As a recruiter for sales people, I was making one placement a month. I started one of your exercises, and today I will have three placements and it is only the 6th of the month!! Total fees are almost $50,000 and I will earn 1/2 of that. Thank you for my new attitude! **Gretchen, California USA**

*Inside these pages lie Ancient laws
that will attach wings to your heart's desire
and make your spirit soar*

How To Be

Wildly
Wealthy
FAST

Sandy Forster

A powerful Step by Step Guide to Attract Prosperity
and Abundance into Your Life TODAY!

www.WildlyWealthy.com

First Australian paperback edition 2004
Second edition February 2005
Third edition May 2005

Sandy@WildlyWealthy.com

Published by

Universal Prosperity Pty Ltd
PO Box 362
Mooloolaba
Qld 4557
Australia
07 5444 6186

For interviews with Sandy Forster for both print and TV, contact -

In Australia: Yvette Adams 07 5493 7899   Mobile 0405 022 977
media@wildlywealthywomen.com

In US: Jan Beasley 970 731 0108
info@wildlywealthy.com

ISBN 0 9752490 0 2

Printed by Queensland Complete Printing Services
28 Price Street, Nambour, Queensland, Australia
www.qprint.com.au

My Deepest Appreciation

It most certainly would have been a much slower path to where I am today without the wonderful support, guidance and generous sharing from my mentors. There are far too many to mention here – so a HUGE 'Thank You' to everyone who has touched my life in some way and helped me become a better person.

I would particularly like to thank Mark Victor Hansen and Robert Allen, best selling authors of *The One Minute Millionaire*, who for years have inspired me to think far bigger than ever before and to believe that financial freedom really was possible for me.

Mike Litman and Jason Oman, authors of *Conversations with Millionaires*, pushed me to 'just get started'. They made me realise that starting small doesn't mean you can't finish big. Without them, I'd still be waiting for 'just the right moment' and jumping from idea to idea.

Esther and Jerry Hicks and *Abraham*, who 'blew my mind' when I discovered their teachings and continue to be a source of inspiration today.

Anthony Robbins, started me on the path of personal development and Candye Hinton was my financial coach when things were tough and was my first step toward financial freedom.

Dr Wayne Dyer opened my eyes to the wonders of the Universe and shared his techniques so I could create the life of my dreams.

Robyn Henderson whose writing workshop was exactly what I needed to take my book out of my head and onto paper.

My wonderful editor Suzanne Dean who encouraged me and went far beyond her job description to save my sanity!

My two dearest friends; Tania, who was my very first prosperity student and is an inspiration for others to always follow their dreams, no matter what life throws at you, and

Melissa, a kindred spirit and soul sister who makes me feel anything is possible!

And the biggest thank you of all... An enormous, gigantic, love-filled thank you to my two beautiful children — Danielle and Dane. They 'enjoyed the ride' (or should I say endured), going through the bad with me to get to the good and watching me make mistake after mistake, until I finally got it right. Dane gives me 100% total unconditional love all day, every day and his spirit continues to calm and centre me.

And most of all, I dedicate this book to Danielle my beautiful free-spirited daughter who is a true driving force in my life. She is my greatest spiritual teacher and continues to give me lessons day by day (I'm a slow learner!), which push me to try harder and achieve more in everything I do. My greatest desire is that my children truly believe — and experience — that anything, and everything, is possible.

Preface

'A journey of a thousand miles begins with a single step.'
LAO TZU

Welcome… and congratulations!

You've just taken the first step to creating a world filled with abundance, riches, wealth, money, prosperity and joy! Sound too good to be true? Sound like there's hard work involved? Well, think again.

There is a secret to getting everything you could ever want in life. It's really simple; in fact, it may be something you have heard about, or understand already. What you are experiencing financially in your life at the present, whether it be riches beyond your wildest dreams or constant money challenges and struggle, is due to principles you may not even be aware of.

There is a law, a Universal Law, which states, "We attract whatever we choose to give our attention to – whether wanted or unwanted". The result of this law is, if you continue to focus on the lack and limitation in your life, you will continue to create and attract more lack and limitation. If you instead focus on the wealth, abundance and prosperity that is already present in your life – no matter how small it may currently be – then you will instead begin to create and attract more wealth, abundance and prosperity.

And if you have absolutely nothing even remotely prosperous occurring in your life to focus on – it doesn't matter. This is the exciting part – you get to use your imagination. You get to 'make it up'. You get to 'pretend'. You get to 'day dream'. You get to 'fake it 'til you make it'.

This is why it really doesn't matter where you are now – through following the steps in this book, you get to create MORE of whatever it is you desire in your life. What FUN!

For some people, this comes naturally; for others (like me) this can be a slow and arduous journey. Through my many money failures, mistakes and unwise decisions when it came to practical money-making steps, I have been fortunate enough to develop a passion for 'what makes people rich'. It is through this passion that I have been able to create my own incredible wealth, and now, share these secrets with you. Enjoy!

Contents

Introduction

'You are a rich and creative spiritual being.
You can never be less than this. You may frustrate your potential.
You may identify with that which is less than what you can be.
But within you now and always is the unborn possibility of a
limitless experience of inner stability and outer treasure, and yours
is the privilege of giving birth to it.
And you will, if you can believe.'
ERIC BUTTERWORTH

What exactly is Wildly Wealthy? **Whatever you want it to be!**
For some, being Wildly Wealthy will mean having the money
to buy their children a new pair of shoes without blowing the
budget. For some it will mean having the funds available to pay
the bills as they come in. For many it will mean getting out of
debt – forever! Others will feel it's being able to travel the world
as often as they like, and for others it will mean the freedom of
never having to work again, safe in the knowledge that their
money is continuing to multiply faster than they can spend it.

And for some (like me) being Wildly Wealthy is all of the
above, as well as – **making choices based on desires and not on
a bank balance** – AND having a whole lot of fun at the same
time!

Being Wildly Wealthy all begins with a state of mind, and
within this book are the secrets you need to achieve whatever it
is Wildly Wealthy means to you!

Before I discovered and applied the prosperity secrets I will
be sharing with you in the following pages, I had previously
made every money mistake in the book (in fact I could have
written that book and a couple of sequels, and probably starred
in the movie too!!). If you think you're a 'money dummy', take

heart. I have experienced every money challenge there is, from starting businesses that went further into debt with each year, investing in the share market and losing the lot, buying an investment property in one of the hottest markets on the planet and selling at a loss, joining an investment club just before it went bankrupt, investing in 'get rich quick schemes' that were really 'lose money quick scams', joining networking companies that folded just as I started to make money, getting financial advice from people who really didn't know what they were talking about, and generally not respecting and taking care of my money.

I made every money mistake possible – except going bankrupt. The only reason I didn't take that option (and boy was it an enticing option at the time) is because I personally wouldn't be able to sleep at night knowing I didn't repay someone to whom I morally and ethically owed money. Looking back, I realise I probably SHOULD have gone bankrupt, and just made the decision myself to pay everyone back when the money began to flow; it would have been so much easier and far less stressful. Oh well, another money mistake to add to my vast array!

Having struggled all my life around money, always getting by (well, actually going backwards most of the time) but never getting ahead, I finally discovered the secrets of drawing Prosperity to me through the power of my subconscious mind and went from an income of around $15,000 a year to bringing in over $150,000 within 12 months! **I thought my money worries would be over, but I was still struggling financially** – all through a lack of skills as to how to manage money successfully, and not having the mindset to continually attract and keep prosperity. This led to my avid research on the subject of Money and how to make it flow to you and make it grow with you.

This book is not just a 'how to' guide – it is my story.

My aim is for others to learn from my failures and my successes and not have to go through the challenges I consistently experienced. I want to **accelerate your path to Prosperity.** <u>If you are ready to accept more wealth into your life, then you're reading the right book.</u>

Now is the time to get excited about having YOUR life filled with health, wealth, happiness, abundance, joy, riches, laughter, prosperity, love and money!

NOW is the time for you to create more abundance in your life than you ever dreamed possible!

 Wildly Wealthy Action Tip

Begin to get excited at the possibilities your future holds.

Go to www.WildlyWealthy.com to get additional free prosperity gifts now!

Where It All Began

*'The real voyage of discovery consists not in seeking
new landscapes but in having new eyes.'*
MARCEL PROUST

As I write this, I gaze out my large windows at the brightly coloured flower beds, the swimming pool, and the lush palm trees swaying in the breeze and watch the sun sparkling on the surface of the beautiful Mooloolah River as it gently flows to the sea.

I live in a beautiful executive home with swimming pool and spa, drive a stylish silver Landrover Freelander, travel overseas whenever I fancy (sometimes eight or nine times a year) attending all the personal development workshops, seminars and events I want and have a lifestyle many people would adore. But it hasn't always been this way – in fact a few short years ago it was quite the opposite.

For many, many, years, I lived in constant struggle. My entire life revolved around money or, more precisely, the lack of it. **Money consumed me; it frustrated me, annoyed me and scared me, and it most definitely eluded me.** When it came to creating wealth, I felt powerless, hopeless, useless and worthless. I knew deep down inside I was a good person, so why was my life such a shambles. What had I done to deserve this? "What was wrong with me???!!!"

After my marriage broke up in 1990, my financial world took a turn for the worse. I had a three-year-old daughter and a six-month-old son, and with the money I received from our property settlement, I took out a small loan and carefully and lovingly designed and built my 'dream house'. My beautiful home was a combination of soothing pastel yellows and blues to remind me of the beach. Full of natural timber and terracotta with lots of big windows to let the sunlight come streaming through, I designed it complete with a freeform palm-fringed pool, western red-cedar French doors with ornate brass handles, and large shady verandahs overlooking the tropical rainforest. My plan was to live in this house until my children left home – but the universe had other ideas.

About a month before construction was complete and I was due to move into my beautiful new home, I was informed that my ex-husband's child support payments would be dropped from the expected $1600 a month to around $100 a month. Now that was a shock! With my own business not making a profit and a now two-year-old son and a five-year-old daughter to look after, I knew this was not a good sign.

Shortly after moving into my beautiful house, I simply couldn't keep up the loan repayments (even with both my sister and parents helping out) and had to put the house on the market. What a sad day that was.

When it was finally time to move out, I remember crying and walking from empty room to empty room saying goodbye. It wasn't just my home I was saying goodbye to – I felt like I was saying goodbye to my dreams. I had hit an all time low. With the money I had left after selling my beautiful home, I made bad investment choice after bad investment choice and eventually ended up over $100,000 in debt.

I was at breaking point. My nerves were shot. I was an impatient, angry, very sad and stressed 'crummy mummy'. I had no idea where my life was going or how I would ever get out of debt. I no longer enjoyed my surf wear business, but had no clue as to what I could possibly do next. The only thing that I enjoyed was personal development. "How on earth could someone make money at that?" I wondered. Little did I know what the Universe had in store for me.

The Magic Pen

'Whatever the mind can conceive and believe, it can achieve.'
NAPOLEON HILL

Two months before moving out of my beautiful home, I remember listening to an audio-program. It talked about the power between the pen and the mind; how writing unleashes a force that is far greater than your actions could ever produce by themselves and why it is so important to write your goals down. The program I was listening to said to **write down your Ideal Day** – so I did!

What a lot of fun that was. How would **my ideal day** look? How would it feel? Now that was easy...

"First", I wrote, "I'd get up in the morning and meditate, do some yoga stretches, and then I'd go for a walk or a run down the beach or a swim in my pool. I'd come home, get the kids off to school and then go to the gym for a workout. Afterwards I would read some inspiring or motivating books to help me to grow and become a better person. Then I would listen to personal development tapes and hopefully I would be able to share what I'd learnt with someone else and make a difference in their lives.

I remember writing all this down and saying to a friend, **"If I was living my ideal day, I'd never have time to make any money"**. Simply being able to live my ideal day was a concept I thought I was not to experience in my lifetime.

Keep in mind, at the time I wrote this down I was over $100,000 in debt and working seven days a week in a business I no longer enjoyed. The only reason I was surviving financially was because I was receiving the sole parent benefit (welfare) from the Government. To say I was fairly stressed about money was a mammoth understatement.

To top it all off I began experiencing physical problems – I needed stitches in a deep slash in my hand, my lower back pain was so bad I was bedridden for days at a time, I detected a lump in my breast and I underwent surgery for cancers on my neck and face that required over 40 big ugly stitches. (It's bad enough feeling like a piece of 'doggie-do' but when you start to look like Frankenstein ... really, how much can one girl take?)

One of the things that I used to keep me sane at the time was listening to Wayne Dyer's *Meditations for Manifesting* CD. It made me feel anything was possible; that I could attract good into my life; that there was still some hope for my dream.

Now fast-forward about six months. I was attending a seminar for a new business I was building. The first day was a 'Business Training' held by some of the leaders in the company. We were told to plan our day if we wanted to be successful and asked to 'Do our homework that night' and fill in the day planner sheet we were given. So because I'm good at following instructions, I went back to my hotel room that night and began filling in the sheet. **Now, how exactly did I spend my time these days?**

Well, firstly, I get up in the morning and meditate, and then I do some yoga and go for a run down the beach. Then after I take the kids to school I go to the gym; then I come home and read some of the personal development products I market and then I listen to some of the tapes. Then I phone people and tell them how great the products are...

Well, as you can imagine, at this point I'm getting chills down my spine and I'm having a total 'Aha!' moment. I remembered writing an identical list down months earlier, thinking it would be an impossibility – and here I was LIVING it. And not only was I living it, I was making around $10,000 a month – almost as much as I would make for an entire year previously!

It was in that moment, sitting on my hotel bed with tears of joy and gratitude running down my face, that I realised, not just in my head but in my HEART, I actually had the power to write the script for my life – that I could actually design my future and I could create it as I wanted it to be.

Now I can't say that from that point on it was all onward and upward with my finances. I still had some huge hurdles to overcome – hurdles that I couldn't see and didn't even know existed; hurdles YOU too may have. These hurdles are the subconscious blocks to your wealth that have probably been with you for life. But what I do know is, if I can overcome my 'poverty consciousness' upbringing and create prosperity in my life – YOU CAN TOO.

As an international Prosperity Coach I have taken thousands of people from around the world through a program I developed called *Millionaire Mindset*. This program consisted of more than 10 hours of intense learning, and really showed people how to transform their life from lack and limitation into unlimited prosperity and **I'm going to show you EXACTLY how to do it too!**

Different By Design

'When everything goes against you,
and it seems you cannot hold on for a minute longer
never give up then, for that is just the time and place
that the tide will turn.'
HARRIET BEECHER STOWE

As you read a book you take in a lot of information and if you're really dedicated you then begin to implement everything you learn and so make enormous changes in your life. But what I've found from experience is, the majority of people begin with high motivation, and then life catches up with them; days go by and slip into weeks, then lapse into months, and they rarely implement everything (or anything) they learn, so not much change occurs in their life. Then when the next book, audio program, seminar, workshop or presentation comes along, they race off and part with their money all over again in the hope that this will be their quick-fix; the one solution that will solve all their money worries and set them financially free.

Don't go down that path again; follow this plan and your life will change forever! This book is full of tips, strategies, information, exercises and secrets with <u>specific steps</u> you can implement on a consistent basis day by day and week by week. In addition to that, I offer Wildly Wealthy Mastermind sessions around the world where I am there to answer all your questions and we can expand on the principles in this book. This way you not only learn the skills to create financial freedom and practise them in your own time, but you also have continuing on-going support from me, and a network of like-minded prosperity-focused individuals from around the world. This reinforces the information I share with you, and for those who are slow learners like I was, <u>it can help you move from 'knowledge in your head</u>

to a knowing in your heart' – and that's when your life will really begin to transform, right in front of your eyes!

It is often said that knowledge is power. Leslie Fieger, who wrote *The Initiation,* said, **"It is the application of knowledge that begets power."**

That's what my aim is for you… I want you to gain power as you change your life and circumstances by applying the methods outlined in these pages.

Many of you will be learning these principles for the very first time, while for others, they will be ideas you have heard or read before, but presented here with a new slant, or I may help you reach a new level of understanding. My desire is that you apply this knowledge and begin to **see real enhancements to your levels of abundance and prosperity**.

Anthony Robbins, a motivating mentor, always says "Repetition is the mother of skill" and that is so true. Through the pages of this book you will learn to master the fundamentals, and if you apply them, over and over again, you will achieve financial freedom, easily and consistently.

In this book, you will find both practical steps AND metaphysical principles such as the Universal Law of Attraction, which utilizes the powerful subconscious mind to help draw people, events and opportunities to you that **will increase your prosperity and level of wealth**.

 Wildly Wealthy Action Tip

Visit www.WildlyWealthy.com to find out more about our Wildly Wealthy Mastermind sessions.

Powerful Secrets

'We are what we think. All that we are arises with our thoughts.
With our thoughts, we make the world.'

BUDDHA

Do NOT underestimate what seems like a simple idea. The secrets I share with you have within them the infinite power of the Universe; the support of something far greater than you – the intelligence and connection and omnipotence of all there was, all there is and all there ever will be. **By embracing just one small secret, you have the potential to transform your life forever!**

For those of you who are new to Universal Laws – the term 'metaphysical' is not some new-age, hocus-pocus, woo-woo. The Metaphysical is simply – 'greater than the physical' or 'beyond the physical' or, as one dictionary definition states, 'a reality beyond what is perceptible to the known senses'.

Although we are aware of and use the senses of touch, taste, smell, sight and sound, we have access to a power far greater than just those five physical senses. It's often said that mankind use around 10% of their brain. It's been proven that we actually use even less than that, so we have around 90% of our brain that we are NOT using at all, and **that 90% is the most powerful, amazing tool we could ever hope to utilise.** I will be sharing with you some techniques that use this part of the brain so you can tap into that incredible force that will transform your world.

In this book I refer to The Metaphysical, and our connection to it, as many things including God, Spirit, Universal Consciousness, Formless Substance, and my favourite term, The Universe.

The reason I combine metaphysical principles to manifest money with practical steps to manage that money, is because I went from $15,000 a year income (sole parent benefit) to making well over

$100,000 in my new personal development business, but I was still struggling financially and realized that you really need both skills combined.

Because I was not managing my money wisely, I discovered that, at some subconscious level, I was saying, 'No, don't let me keep it; I don't know how to handle money; I'm not good with money' – **so I was pushing it out of my experience.**

That's when I became very scared. I thought once I was bringing in good money, my financial worries would be over – but they were just magnified. I began to think money didn't like me, so I continued to be afraid, worried and stressed when it came to money. I knew something had to change. I wanted my connection with money to change. I was sick and tired of the dysfunctional relationship I had with money. I wanted to feel at peace with money. I wanted to embrace money. I wanted to spend quality time with money. I wanted to feel in my heart that "I love money and money loves me".

By embracing just one small secret, you have the potential to transform your life forever!

So I studied everything I possibly could around how to live a life of prosperity and abundance and the first thing I discovered was: **if you consistently think and feel wealthy, you will become wealthy. It HAS to happen**. So how do you do that?

 Wildly Wealthy Action Tip
Read on to discover how YOU can become Wildly Wealthy.

Let the Journey Begin...

*'When science begins the study of non-physical phenomena,
it will make more progress in one decade
than in all the previous centuries of its existence.'*

NIKOLA TESLA

Quantum physics has now proved that everything in the Universe is vibrating. If you could get the biggest, strongest microscope in the world and put a rock, or a piece of wood, or a chair, or a pillow, a leaf or a flower — anything at all, whether living or inanimate— under that microscope, you would see tiny energy particles or packets vibrating together. Everything is made of tiny vibrating energy packets. That is true of EVERYTHING in our Universe, including our thoughts and our words.

The interesting thing is, when we think a thought, or speak our words, **the energy or vibration that makes up that thought or word goes out and attracts a like vibration and brings that back into our world.**

> *Get excited as your life is about to change forever.*

Our thoughts are like radio waves or frequencies, or vibrations or energy going out into the world. **That energy or vibration goes out and attracts a like vibration or energy and brings that back into our world.**

So, if you have your mind and thoughts set to 'lack and limitation', that's the signal you send out. It then picks up similar signals or vibrations, which come back to you, drawing into your life that same lack and limitation. And then you wonder why your life continues with the same old patterns and results year after year.

Whereas, if you are focused on riches, abundance, prosperity and wealth, that's the signal you send out and that's what you will attract back into your world. **What you are focusing on most of the time will be made perfectly clear to you** (and everybody else – how embarrassing!!) **by what is showing up in your world.**

To put it in the words of many others:

◊ What you focus on, is what you create

◊ As ye think, so shall ye be

◊ Like attracts like

◊ Change your thoughts, change your world

◊ What you think about is what you create

◊ You become what you think about all day long.

So if you are not living a life of abundance and riches, you have to change what you think about most of the time. You have to change what is called your dominant vibration.

So how do you do that?

Well, you've come to the right place. In this book you will discover dozens of ways to help you <u>change your dominant vibration by focusing on prosperity and wealth</u> **so you begin to attract more of it into your life – easily.** So read on!

 Wildly Wealthy Action Tip

Get excited – your life is about to change forever!

Creating Your Millionaire Mindset

'The ownership of money and property comes as a result of doing things in a certain way. Those who do things in this certain way, whether on purpose or accidentally, get rich.
Those who do not do things in this certain way, no matter how hard they work or how able they are, remain poor.
It is a natural law that like causes always produce like effects.
Therefore, any man or woman who learns to do things in this certain way will infallibly get rich'

WALLACE D. WATTLES

The first step in achieving Abundance is changing the way you THINK around money. Think like a Millionaire so you BECOME a Millionaire. **This very first step to creating the prosperity you desire is definitely the most fun!**

Everything that comes into physical reality is first 'formless' – it is actually floating all around us, but not yet solid enough to be seen. You can tap into this formless substance through your mind. That is how you place the order for what you want. <u>Holding an idea in your mind will cause it to appear in your physical world.</u> Too often, you are thinking of what you don't want – which causes the thing you don't want to actually happen and then you wonder WHY things don't change year after year. **Change your thoughts and you change your world!**

We've all heard of people who have nothing then win the lottery and become Millionaires – only to find a few years later they are back to nothing, and quite often have even less money than before they won the lottery. Conversely, how many times do you hear of a

Millionaire who experiences a downturn in the market, or makes a bad business decision, or goes into bankruptcy and loses the lot – only to find a few years later, they're back to being a Millionaire. This is because one person has a Millionaire Mindset and one doesn't. So I challenge you – where is YOUR mindset? <u>Do you have a prosperity consciousness or a poverty consciousness?</u>

Now at this point, you can tell me whatever story you like. You can explain about your background and your past 'horror stories'; you can share with me all the reasons why you do have a prosperity consciousness, but the money just hasn't shown up yet.

You can make up whatever you like about why you're not rich right now, but the truth of the matter is – <u>if you are struggling financially, it's because you think MORE about financial struggle than being wealthy.</u>

If you're broke right now, it's because you think MORE about being broke than living a life of financial freedom. If you have no money right now, it's because you think MORE about having no money than being a Millionaire. And because you are thinking about financial struggle, being broke or having no money, your thoughts expand into feelings. Then you feel – emotionally and physically – that you don't have enough, and **when you feel** you don't have enough, you continue to CREATE not having enough. **So just by continually giving that attention to where your life is right NOW, you continue to re-create that same life over and over.**

> *Change your thoughts and you change your world.*

But never fear – that's why I'm here. Just by making the decision to read this book, you have shown that you are ready to make a commitment to yourself to re-create your financial future, and have it look the way YOU want it to. <u>You have set a powerful force in motion that you may not even be aware of right now – so look out – you WILL be prosperous,</u> that's why we also cover the basics of how to handle your money so you can make the most of that flow of abundance that you are about to tap into.

Wildly Wealthy Action Tip

Begin to imagine yourself as already Wildly Wealthy!

Go to www.WildlyWealthy.com to get your free prosperity resources now.

Turbo Charge Your Prosperity

'Success isn't a result of spontaneous combustion.
You must set yourself on fire.'
ARNOLD GLASCOW

You can read this book and say – "Yep, great book, great information, knew a lot of that already – I'll start using some of those tips soon". Or, you can turbo-charge your path to prosperity by **actually applying the secrets in this book as you go.**

Wildly Wealthy Action Tips are sprinkled throughout this book and if you want the most exciting results and FAST, apply them now in your life and watch your finances improve – it's that easy! I highly recommend reading this book more than once. Read it from cover to cover and then slowly and deliberately read one chapter each day, applying each Wildly Wealthy Action Tip as you go.

If you snooze, you lose, but if you choose to turbo-charge your way to wealth, you must buy a ring binder from an office supplies store and a hole-punch. You can decorate this in any way you desire – my first Prosperity binder was decorated with photocopied money (until I found out it was HIGHLY illegal to print money. Whoops – don't try that one at home!).

I'd like you to use your Prosperity binder to keep all your exercises and notes together, so you can refer to it at any time. If you're asked to do an exercise or write something out – put it in your Prosperity Binder. You can dig it out when you need to focus on wealth and you will be able to add to it as you find other great tips on prosperity. **You will find your Prosperity Binder becomes a cherished resource for all things prosperous.**

Don't feel you have to implement every strategy, exercise, secret and tip I share with you every single day. The idea is to make this FUN! The more fun you have, the easier it will be to attract the things you desire into your life. So whilst I don't recommend doing everything every day, <u>I do recommend doing something every day and, obviously, the more you do, the faster and more effective your results will be.</u>

It's a little like dieting. You can learn how to lift weights, how to run, how to eat less, how to eat healthy foods, how to do yoga and how to exercise, but you wouldn't have to do all of the above every single day to lose weight. You would be expected to do at least one activity every day and if you incorporated a couple of these things into your day, your results would surely be more spectacular.

It's exactly the same with manifesting all the abundance, prosperity, riches and wealth you desire – you don't have to do everything every day, but for the best results, <u>do whatever you can, and do it DAILY!</u>

 Wildly Wealthy Action Tips

Purchase and decorate your Prosperity Binder.

Apply at least ONE tip a day to transform your life.

What's in Your Warehouse?

'Desire is God tapping at the door of your mind,
trying to give you greater good.
That you deeply desire something is positive proof
that it has already been prepared for you,
and is only waiting for you to recognize and accept it.'
CATHERINE PONDER

To further explain the above quote, I want you to picture this in your mind — way out there in the Universe, **floating somewhere in space, is a huge warehouse with YOUR name on it.** In that warehouse is everything you have ever wanted, everything you desire now, and everything you will ever want. It's all there for the taking. And the only reason you have a desire, or wish or dream about something, is because it's in your warehouse waiting for you to order it.

Now when I say 'order it', I mean make it a 'standing order'. What usually happens is, you have a desire (you place your order) then you come up with all the reasons you won't ever have, achieve or get that desire (you cancel the order). Let's say you see a picture of a really cool car, the car of your dreams, and you think to yourself – oh yes, one day I'm going to have one of those. You start imagining how wonderful you will feel when you own one. You see yourself in the car, picture yourself behind the wheel and feel how good it feels to own the car and drive it around.

At that point, all the little 'helpers' in your warehouse start running around excitedly shouting, **"She's put in the order for the car – she wants her car! Quick, let's deliver it"**– and they slide the warehouse door open and back the delivery truck in. They open the truck's rear door, put the ramp in place and start pushing your new car up the ramp and into the delivery truck.

Now, if in the next breath you say to yourself, "But I can't possibly afford that car; I'll never save enough to buy it", <u>you have in that moment 'cancelled your order'</u>. So what happens next is, all your little helpers look sad and say, "She's cancelled her order again; take it out", and they wheel your beautiful new car out of the delivery truck and back into your warehouse.

Then maybe you're driving around in your old bomb and you see someone driving around in that beautiful car that you want. And you go to the newsagents and buy a magazine with a picture of your car, and you cut it out and stick it on your computer. You look at it every day. You go for a test drive at the local car dealer and you get yourself feeling that it's possible again. And sure enough, your warehouse once again is a hive of activity. They're running around. Your new car is in the back of the delivery truck and they're locking the rear door. They turn the key in the ignition. The motor kicks over and then… You have a 'hiccup' in your life. You have a bad day, get an unexpected bill, or have a fight with your partner and you think, as you look at the picture of your new car, "I'll never get one of those; nothing ever works out for me; life's hard". And in that moment, you've just cancelled your order again – they turn off the truck's ignition, open the back door and roll your beautiful car back into your warehouse.

You have no idea how many times your desires are in and out, in and out, in and out and back into your warehouse. If you have thoughts or a desire that you want something, it's because it's in your warehouse. When you come up with all the reasons why you can't have it, you cancel your order. And the part of you that comes up with those reasons is your saboteur – your logical mind. Now don't get me wrong, the logical mind is a wonderful thing, it's just that when it comes to attracting or manifesting what you desire, **it's the one thing that will stop you or hold you back from living the life of your dreams.**

So, during these processes I share with you, just take the time to disengage the logical mind. Take the time to <u>use your imagination like a child again, where anything is possible, where you have no limitations, where you believe you can and will get whatever you want</u>. Just for the next month, I want you to believe that all the secrets I share with you DO work (which they do) that you CAN attract anything you want (which you can) and that you WILL transform your life (which is exactly what will happen if you allow it).

So how will this work? Well, in the pages of this book you will learn dozens of secrets – which actually aren't even secrets. **The real secret is that you probably don't understand just how powerful these tips and strategies are**, so keep reading as all will be revealed!

 Wildly Wealthy Action Tip

Get excited when a desire comes to mind – **it's in your warehouse**!

Your Intention Sharpens Your Attention

'To know is nothing at all; to imagine is everything.'
ANATOLE FRANCE

I want you to ask yourself, do your finances burden or scare you? Do you consistently not have enough, or are consumed with fear that you won't have enough to live your life the way you want. Whether you desire $50,000 a year, $250,000 a year or even a million dollars a year, everyone's desires are different, it's ALL achievable. **If one person in this world has been able to create riches beyond their wildest dreams, then it is possible for YOU too!**

You must keep in mind that your financial troubles are simply temporary. No matter what situation you are in, you can find the path to freedom – not just financial freedom, but freedom from the stress and worry that really does impact on every other area of your life.

What I'd like you to do today is spend about 15-30 minutes writing down in your Prosperity Binder, your intention for reading this book. What are you expecting to achieve in the next 60 to 180 days? What would you like to see different and what would you like to attract into your life in the next two to six months? Take one step further – how would you like your life to look in one year's time, what would be different? You must be clear and specific about what you're aiming for. <u>The more specific you are, the more likely it is that you'll achieve it.</u>

The secret is, don't think so big that you don't believe it's possible in any way. The idea is to think big enough so that, while it may be a stretch, part of you can actually imagine it happening (even if you have no idea HOW it will happen). **You don't want to think** so big <u>that you feel it's impossible;</u> that you not only stretch, but stretch so far you snap.

For example: let's say you don't own your own business and never have, and you write down you want to own 5 small businesses in the next 6 months that each bring you a profit of $5000 a month. Whilst this is definitely achievable and **the Universe can easily make this and even more happen,** if it is too big a stretch for you mentally and you <u>don't believe it yourself – it's not going to happen</u>. But, on the other hand, if there is a part of you that believes it is achievable (and even much more than this) then go for it! <u>You can never out-dream the Universe</u>, its plans for you are far grander than you could ever imagine.

If you're ready to accept far more in your life, a great exercise to stretch your limits is to **first imagine something far beyond anything you currently believe is possible**. For instance, when I was setting up one of my new ventures, I knew that if I could just get some local, and possibly national media exposure, the business would expand rapidly. So I first began to think about being on Oprah in the US. <u>Now that WAS a huge stretch</u>. That idea was so far off the planet it was in a whole different stratosphere!! The

> *If one person in this world has been able to create riches beyond their wildest dreams, then it is possible for YOU too.*

great thing was, when I focused on being on Oprah long enough, and then came back to thinking about getting media coverage here in Australia – it seemed so much more achievable; it was only a stretch and not a snap. And the bonus is, the Universe heard it all. Not only did I appear on local and national TV, I was also featured internationally! I've even spoken with Oprah's producers about appearing on her show in the future – so stay tuned – **and think big!**

There are no limits to what the Universe can provide; <u>your only limitations are within your own mind</u>. In this exercise you are learning to think outside the box and dream bigger than before. Don't hold back, thing bigger, dream grander, and know **the Universe is waiting to give you your heart's desires**. Remember, you don't have to know HOW you will achieve these things, just go within and feel deep within your soul what you would LOVE to see happen in your life.

Include things such as:

◇ The **amount of money** you would like to be making each month

◇ The **way your life would be different** if you were making that much money

◇ What you would be **doing differently** each day

◇ **How you would feel** if you were making that sort of money

◇ Something specific you want in your life eg. a new house, car, job, holiday, lover etc

◇ **Imagine how you would feel** if you already had that thing in your life right now

Just by doing this exercise, your **intention** is going to sharpen your **attention** and <u>you will be more likely to notice the people, events and circumstances that appear in your life to help you achieve your financial goals.</u>

 Wildly Wealthy Action Tips

Stretch your imagination beyond what you currently believe is possible.

Write down the reason you are reading this book and what you would like to achieve over the next two to six months.

Go to <u>www.WildlyWealthy.com</u> to get your Wildly Wealthy FAST Companion Workbook now.

Abundance In a Minute

'A world of abundance surrounds you,
if only you will step up and claim it.
Make life happen through you rather than letting it happen to you.
It will make all the difference in the world.'
RALPH MARSTON

A surprisingly simple but amazingly powerful exercise to attract prosperity to you takes less than a minute a day, and if you do this daily, you'll be amazed at what you begin to attract into your life. This exercise is called Abundance Breaths and basically all you need to do is breathe. Well, actually, it's a little more than that…

As already stated, you become what you focus on. Too often, it can be challenging to know exactly what you do want. You get caught up in trying to make up your mind - "Do I want this or that? What if I get that and I really would have preferred this?" "I thought I wanted this, but now I think I want that". Sometimes it's easier if you can just **focus on the feeling of abundance**, rather than the specifics of what that abundance will be. It is <u>the feeling that has the attraction power</u> anyway. You can get specific when all the money comes in!

What you should do before this exercise to create avalanches of abundance and prosperity is find a comfy chair and sit down with your feet flat on the floor, back straight and hands resting in your lap with palms facing up. Gently close your eyes and keep them closed.

Before you get started just imagine that you are now surrounded by tiny, minute particles of abundance; **that you are immersed in a sea of prosperity and you can reach out and touch it and bring it into your life whenever you desire** (which you can!).

When you're ready, take a long, slow, deep Abundance Breath in to the count of three, totally expanding and filling your lungs. Imagine all the while that you are breathing in those particles of prosperity and they are filling every fibre of your being. Feel that feeling of being flooded with abundance. Hold your breath for the count of nine and feel every atom, every cell in your entire body being plumped up with prosperity, filled with abundance, vibrating with riches. And then slowly, to the count of six, breathe out that Abundance to circulate throughout the Universe – really force all that air out.

Once again, take another long, slow, deep Abundance Breath in, and this time, see your body light up from the inside out, glowing with prosperity, sparkling with riches, dazzling with wealth. I like to imagine that my body is glowing from the inside out with that same golden glow that radiates from Scrooge McDuck's millions, or the gold in Aladdin's cave! Once again, hold for the count of nine, seeing that glow, feeling that glow, then on the out breath, once again breathe out the abundance to circulate throughout the Universe.

"Feel how it feels to be rich beyond your wildest dreams!"

One last time, slowly breathe in a huge big Abundance Breath for the count of three, and while you hold that breath for the count of nine, **imagine and feel** what it's like to be totally abundant, amazingly wealthy, to have achieved financial freedom and be rich beyond your wildest dreams. Feel how that feels; feel how light and free and good that feels. Expand that feeling; feel it flood through your body. Embrace that amazing feeling throughout your body, mind and spirit. And for the last time, slowly breathe that abundance and prosperity out to circulate throughout the Universe. And when you're ready, slowly open your eyes, feeling prosperous, feeling wealthy, feeling rich, rich, rich!

As I said, this is a very easy, very powerful little trick you can do daily or many times, if you want to attract MORE into your life.

It only takes a couple of minutes, but has amazing money-magnetizing powers. Once you get really good at your Abundance Breaths, you won't even need to close your eyes – you will be able to feel those feelings, see your body glowing with prosperity and really feel you are beginning to attract money anytime, anywhere – what fun!

 Wildly Wealthy Action Tip

Practise your Abundance Breaths.

Go to www.WildlyWealthy.com to listen to an audio of these powerful Abundance Breaths.

Change Your Focus, Change Your Life

'Of all the creatures of earth, only human beings can change their patterns. Man alone is the architect of his destiny. Human beings, by changing the inner attitudes of their minds, can change the outer aspects of their lives.'
WILLIAM JAMES

As you've already learnt, what you focus on is what you then create in your life. One of the fastest ways to change your life is to change your focus. I have discovered that one of the easiest ways to do that is to have what I call a 'Media Blackout'.

If you sat down and counted how many hours you spend listening to the radio, reading newspapers or magazines and watching TV – you might be horrified. Let's say you do nothing more than skim through the daily paper, listen to the radio on the way to and from work, read a magazine every lunch break, then come home, watch the evening news and two of your favourite shows every day. This alone means you could be spending around three to five hours a day focusing on **other people's lives,** things that are <u>not</u> helping you to create **your** ideal life.

Now if you took just two, or even one, of those hours daily and applied some of the tips in this book, believe me – <u>your life would change forever – guaranteed</u>. It's just a matter of doing it, not just reading it. So turn off the idiot box, throw away those trashy magazines, cancel your newspaper delivery and get busy focusing on how you want YOUR life to be, not on how others are living theirs! In the pages of this book you will find dozens of ways to begin designing your life.

Don't underestimate this step – it will have a huge impact. You might be surprised to see how addicted you are to TV, papers etc.

Even if you can't do without them for a lifetime, just try it for a month. For those of you who are worried you are going to look like an ignorant fool – **don't worry**. Although I try to remain blissfully unaware of the disasters and bad news stories that usually appear in the media, I find there are many 'helpful' people who keep me up-to-date with all the drama that is going on in the world – so you won't miss much.

> *You will achieve more, become wealthier, live a life far beyond anything you could imagine.*

And by the way, I'm not TOTALLY disconnected. I watch my favourite show every Saturday night and occasionally sit down and watch something with my kids. I try to limit myself to no more than two hours a week – I find that's plenty and I know I get so much more done without it.

If you really have to know what's going on in other people's lives – standing in a supermarket queue is a great way to catch up on the latest gossip in those trashy mags. Doesn't take up any extra time (and doesn't cost a thing) and you can usually skim through from cover to cover in about five minutes flat and be totally up-to-date with who's currently sleeping with whom, who's now divorced and what the latest and greatest fashions are, if you really want to know!

<u>You will achieve more, become wealthier, live a life far beyond anything you could imagine, if you just spent more time focusing on what YOU want to create</u>, rather than what others have created, or what is currently going on in the world. You get to choose – the life of YOUR dreams, or someone else's dream?

 Wildly Wealthy Action Tips

Turn off the TV and switch off the radio.

Throw away those magazines and newspapers.

Begin feeding your mind with positive thoughts, images and sounds that keep you focused on what you DO want to attract into your life.

The Three-Minute Money Marvel

'Gratitude unlocks the fullness of life.
It turns what we have into enough, and more...
Gratitude makes sense of our past,
brings peace for today,
and creates a vision for tomorrow.'
MELODY BEATTIE

In this day and age, (gosh, I sound like my grandmother!) it's easy to get so caught up living day-to-day that we don't take a moment to really appreciate what we already have in our lives. There's nothing wrong with wanting more, desiring bigger, dreaming grander – as long as you take the time to **recognise how wonderful your life already is.**

One of my mentors once said, "There are billions of people, right now, all around the world, who – **if they could swap places with you for just one day** – would be living a life so far beyond anything they could have ever imagined. Your day-to-day life is their wildest dreams come true and much, much more."

Now rather than just read that sentence, <u>I want you to really feel it</u>; think about those people and imagine they DO have your life for a day – no matter how dismal you think your life is. **Imagine how amazed and grateful they would feel each moment for all the things you experience on a daily basis**– a roof over your head, a bed to sleep in, food and drinks, clean water, a safe environment. Just imagine how they would feel in that moment – do you think grateful may be one of the words to describe their emotions?

Well, gratitude has to be an integral step on your journey to a life of Abundance. You simply will not experience all the richness you desire without expressing gratitude on a daily basis.

In her book *Simple Abundance*, Sarah Ban Breathnach says, "You simply will not be the same person two months from now after consciously giving thanks each day for the abundance that exists in your life. And you will have set in motion an ancient spiritual law: The more you have and are grateful for, the more will be given you".

I have found that a Gratitude Journal, or Grateful Journal, is the best way to do this. Basically, what you do is take a blank journal or notebook (you can decorate it if you wish) and at the end of every day, just before you go to sleep, reflect on your day. Take the time to write down at least five things that have occurred that you can be grateful for. Now these don't have to be earth shattering, mind blowing, incredible events – it can be as simple as "I am so grateful I watched the sunrise this morning because the oranges and the pinks splashed across the clouds were beautiful"; or, "I am so grateful for the wind and the way it makes the trees dance"; or, "I am grateful that I tidied my desk and have some space to work without clutter"; or, "I'm grateful I found a $20 note in the pocket of my old jeans". Sometimes if you've had a day you'd rather forget, you may write what I once did: "I am so grateful today is over and I'm going to bed"!

Something wonderful begins to happen when you use a Grateful Journal. At first, you may be like me and you'll just be *nodding off to sleep* when suddenly you sit bolt upright in bed, grab your journal and think – "goodness – what happened to me today that I can be grateful for?" Then over time, certain things will happen during the day and *immediately afterwards* you will think, "That would be a good thing to write in my Grateful Journal".

Then you'll find things will happen during your day and you'll think **in the moment** – "Oh, I can be grateful for this" and you'll start to feel those feelings of gratitude on a more consistent basis. Then as time goes by, you'll begin to find yourself *looking for things* to be grateful for. And guess what, whatever you look for, whatever you give your attention to, whatever you focus on, you will then begin to see more of in your life.

So there'll come a time when there will be a whole shift in your focus. As you continually look for things to be grateful for, **you'll find so many more things begin to appear in your life and start occurring, for you to be grateful for.**

I remember one of my clients coming back to me the week after I had shared this strategy and saying, "Sandy, I had a Grateful Journal. I used it all the time, but then my husband had a car accident and life got busy and I just stopped using it. After our last session I decided to find my journal and searched high and low. I finally found it and as I put it in my hands, it naturally fell open, and in the pages of the journal was $500 cash. I must have put it there years ago and forgotten about it". Well, she certainly had something to write about in her Grateful Journal that night!

A Grateful Journal makes a WONDERFUL gift. I made one for my daughter years ago when I was a money mess. I bought a $2 notebook from Crazy Clarks (a discount store). I purchased some brightly coloured markers and a gold pen and decorated every page within that journal with inspiring quotes, or things I was grateful for about her, or things I loved about her. Every page that didn't have something written on it, I put a cute sticker. It was a wonderful present and she used it all the time. It didn't cost much at all, but **it's a powerful gift to give someone** – not just the present, but what that gift will do to their life when they begin using it.

Also, once you've actually created your own measure of financial freedom, don't ever take it for granted. When I was overseas launching Wildly Wealthy Women in New Zealand, I was booked into a beautiful hotel in the middle of Auckland. When I arrived in my room (the penthouse on the 28th floor) the first thing I did was check the whole place out. In the main room was a huge king-sized bed, an over-sized TV and state-of-the-art stereo system. The walk-in robe was big enough to fit enough clothes for a year. One wall of my room was made up entirely of sliding glass doors that led out to a balcony overlooking Auckland's beautiful harbour and there was a telescope perched there if I wanted a closer peek at anything.

When I walked into the bathroom, my mouth fell open. It was floor to ceiling marble in black and white. There was a huge oval spa bath, two hand basins with ceiling-high mirrors and a special make-up area. In the corner was a beautiful display of grey river rocks and in the opposite corner was an amazing shower with seven nozzles (yes you read that right, seven) for the most incredible massage shower you have ever experienced. Now when I entered that room, I didn't just think, "How beautiful, aren't I lucky", in an appropriate grown up show of appreciation. Oh no, I wanted the Universe to know just how grateful I was. I jumped up and down; I squealed with delight; I did a little happy dance; I clapped my hands with joy. I said, "Thank you, thank you, thank you" to the Universe. **I know where my good comes from and I make sure I display physically the emotions I feel inside** – I let it all hang out!

Let me tell you, this CAN sometimes be embarrassing, because I simply cannot hide my emotions – I let it fly (good and bad) and think about it later. Yes, I realise thinking first and then acting later is the more mature way to behave but I've got a little girl in me bursting to get out and she does so at every possible opportunity. This often makes me look a little crazy, a little ditzy, even a little silly – but guess what? I'm living the life of my dreams and I'm happy, happy, happy.

> *"Be who you are and say what you feel,*
> *because those who mind don't matter,*
> *and those who matter don't mind."*
>
> Dr. Seuss

So don't let others' opinions of your actions stop you from enjoying life the way YOU want to. <u>Be grateful for what you have and let it show in any way you like.</u>

 Wildly Wealthy Action Tips

Begin writing in your grateful journal TODAY! Show your gratitude in any way that feels good to you.

An Attitude of Gratitude

'Feeling grateful or appreciative of someone or something
in your life, actually attracts more of the things
that you appreciate and value
into your life.'
CHRISTIANE NORTHRUP

Gratitude is your key to riches. Gratitude will immediately start expanding your energy and your life! Once you begin to use your Grateful Journal on a daily basis **your life will change forever**. Why not start right now and begin a list of 25 things that you are grateful for already!

1. _____

2. _____

3. _____

4. _____

5. _____

6. _____

7. _____

8. _____

9. _____

10. _____

11. _____

12. _____

13. _____

14. _____

15. _____

16. _____

17. _____

18. _____

19. _____

20. _____

21. _____

22. _____

23. _____

24. _____

25. _____

 *Wildly Wealthy Action Tip*
Complete this list immediately!

Why Wealthy?

'You can't get thin from hating being fat.
And you cannot attract prosperity from disliking being poor.'
ABRAHAM-HICKS

You are not doing anyone any favour, least of all yourself, by remaining poor. You must begin to think bigger and expand your comfort zone when it comes to wealth. Get used to the idea of unlimited wealth in your life. Feel the joy of abundance and riches flooding your daily existence. **When you feel at one with the idea of greater prosperity – that's when you will see it appear in your life.** As with any Universal Law, if you follow it – the outcome is exact. You cannot fail. Therefore, if you follow the strategies outlined in this book, it HAS to happen.

What would being wealthy mean to you? Would it be flashy cars, houses around the world, would you be dripping in gold jewellery and furs? Or would it be living your life with purpose and being able to make a difference in other people's lives because you have the time and money available to make it happen. It really doesn't matter why

> *When you feel at one with the idea of greater prosperity – that's when you will see it appear in your life.*

you want to be rich, there is no right or wrong. **The Universe wants you to be rich and that's all that matters!**

Too often people feel they don't deserve to have more, or more precisely, don't deserve to have more than others. They think if they have more, someone will miss out. They feel guilty that their family, their friends, their neighbours, or even people around the world they have never even met, will have less than them. Nothing could be further from the truth.

The Universe desires you to have everything you want. The Universe will continue to create everything you and everyone else desires out of 'formless substance'. No one will go without because you have more, no one will miss out because you learn how to tap into the unlimited flow of prosperity. **You will create more.**

When you plant seeds in your garden and tend to your flowerbed, do you feel a sense of guilt because your neighbour will have to go without flowers? Do you feel uneasy because your parents have fewer flowers than you and you feel you've taken more than your fair share? Of course not! You know they have the ability to plant those same seeds and create those same beautiful flowers – as could any person around the world if they followed the same steps as you. It's exactly the same with money. Once you have the formula, once you know how to plant those abundance seeds, you can create as much as you wish. And anyone else following that same formula will also be able to create as much as they wish. And if everyone in the entire world were to use that same formula, then **everyone would be rich beyond their wildest dreams**. No one goes without; more is created. Flowers or money — it's all the same!

I recall years ago reading that only 5% of the people on the planet control 95% of the world's wealth. Which means everyone else on the planet – the other 95% – is controlling only 5% of the world's wealth. Which end of the scale are you? **Which end would you like to be?** It's also been said that if all the money throughout the entire world was equally redistributed among every person on the planet there is enough wealth for each man, woman and child to be a millionaire. And even if that occurred, within six months they say, the money would be back in the same hands it came from. This is because money – like all events and experiences – comes to us, not by economics or fate or because of our upbringing, but **by what we are thinking; by our consciousness**. And this book is exactly what you need to change your consciousness forever!

There is much more money and wealth in the world than most people ever realize, and you can create even more if you want more! Don't feel guilty that you will be taking from others – **you**

will be an inspiration to others. Just continue to focus on wealth and more will come to you. Focusing on others with less than you, trying to help them, spending time with them will NOT make them rich – but it may make you poor.

As stated in *The Science of Getting Rich* by Wallace D. Wattles, "You are not deserting the poor in their misery when you refuse to allow your mind to be filled with pictures of that misery. Poverty can be done away with, not by increasing the number of well-to-do people who think about poverty, but by increasing the number of poor people whose purpose with faith is to get rich. **The poor do not need charity; they need inspiration**. Charity only sends them a loaf of bread to keep them alive in their wretchedness, or gives them an entertainment to make them forget for an hour or two. But inspiration can cause them to rise out of their misery. If you want to help the poor, demonstrate to them that they can become rich. <u>Prove it by getting rich yourself.</u>"

Be a guiding light to others and show them how to create a life filled with prosperity and abundance!

 Wildly Wealthy Action Tip

Get rich and be an inspiration to others.

Pay the Person Who Will Make You Rich

*'More people should learn to tell their dollars where to go,
instead of asking them where they went.'*
ROBERT BABSON

To really be open to accepting avalanches of abundance in your life, you MUST begin to implement some practical steps as well. It's all very well to go off to a mountaintop and meditate on manifesting your wealth, but **unless you take some practical steps**, NOTHING much will change. I have discovered the Universe loves order, particularly so around money. If you can't manage the small amount you bring in now, how confident do you think the Universe feels about sending you millions? How confident do you feel about managing millions?

Of all the practical strategies we cover, this step is vital to creating great Wealth. <u>You already know someone who will make you rich</u>. In fact, you see this person every day. This is one person you MUST acquaint yourself with if you are to achieve long-term wealth in your life, rather than fleeting abundance. This person is YOU. You and only you are responsible for creating your wealth. And the good thing is, now you are discovering the wealth formula; and we're going to make this as much fun as possible by implementing the practical steps (boring, but oh so important) with the metaphysical steps (fun, fun, fun!) **Put the two together and you have the perfect recipe for wealth!**

I could teach you all the metaphysical steps in the world, but unless you become responsible with your money, it will continue to slip through your fingers and down the drain. If you are not responsible with the money you have, you are, at some subconscious level, <u>pushing more money out of your experience</u>.

Two things happen when you refuse to take responsibility for your money - either you fail to attract it into your life altogether, or if you do attract it, it quickly disappears again.

You must learn to respect money. Do you think someone you treat badly, don't pay attention to and disrespect is going to want to spend time with you? NO! Well it's the same with money. **Money is filled with the same energy that you are**, and if you want more money in your life, <u>you must love and respect the money you already have!</u>

The thing you must begin to do immediately is – **Pay Yourself First.** What I mean by that is, take into account all the money that comes into your life – everything including money from a job, a business, gifts, interest, inheritance etc. The VERY FIRST thing you must do, is put aside 10% of that money into a special account. Now you can call that account anything you like – your Millionaire Account, your Financial Freedom Account, your Wildly Wealthy Account – it doesn't matter what you call it, the main thing is that you put that money aside and do not take it out under any circumstances, <u>unless you are investing it to make **more money.**</u>

> *If you want more money in your life, you must love and respect the money you already have!*

The reason you do this is three-fold. Firstly, putting cash in the bank on a regular basis, no matter how big or small the amounts, seems to free up the energy you hold around money. It loosens things up a little; with cash in the bank you tend to feel a little richer and in doing that, **you allow more of that abundance stream to flow to you.**

Secondly, no matter how much money you make in your job, business or main income source, you will never be totally financially free until you have a passive income (that's money that keeps coming in whether or not you are working) equal to or greater than the income you make from your current job or business. The easiest way to create that passive income is by investing. Now that word alone may scare you off due to past experiences or lack of knowledge. But do not fear – **I will guide you in the right direction.**

The easiest way to put that money aside is to set it up automatically through the bank (via direct debit) – have the money taken out of your pay or a current account and put directly into your special savings account. When you have enough set aside you can start to think about how you would like to invest it or how you would like to make it multiply through starting a profitable business, or investing in real estate or the stock market. You can get more information on investment opportunities at www.WildlyWealthy.com

But the exciting thing about that money is, it's not the money itself that will make you Rich – **it's what that money is going to do**…

 Wildly Wealthy Action Tip

Put 10% of all the money that comes into your life into a separate account to be used to set you Financially Free.

The Eighth Wonder Of the World

'Compound interest – the most powerful force in the Universe.'
ALBERT EINSTEIN

That little bit you save week after week may not seem like much, **but there is a miracle happening every day you may not have heard about**. And that miracle is called Compound Interest. Einstein called compound interest the Eighth Wonder of the World. And indeed he should. Generally speaking, all money knows how to do is to multiply. If you have money and then let it do its thing, it will make more and more for you, it will continue to grow, expand and increase.

To understand the magic of compound interest, let me explain it with this tale:

Let's say back in 1500 Sir William Thatcher (played by cute Heath Ledger in *A Knights Tale*) decided he was going to save for retirement. He had one cent, and he knew he could earn 6% on his money every single year. He put his penny in a special money pouch and placed the interest in his right pocket for safekeeping. He never added anything to the original penny in his pouch, yet the interest continued to accumulate year after year in his right pocket.

William is a supersonically healthy guy and lives until today, 2004 (504 years later) and then decided to retire. So he took his one penny from his money pouch and added it to the simple interest in his right pocket. Guess how much William had? Well, the interest in his right pocket added up to only 30c (1c x 6% x 504 years = 30c) Along with his original cent from his left pocket he has 31c on which to retire. Not very good long-term planning, William!

What could he have done differently? Let's assume William had read some books on investing and knew about compounding. Instead of putting the interest in his right pocket, he put it into his money pouch with the original penny – the principal. **He added the interest to the original penny, so he was getting interest on his interest, on his interest, and on and on over time**. Over the years he would earn that same 6% interest on the original penny PLUS the accumulated interest that he kept putting back into his growing money pouch (he's compounding the interest).

The story may have started off much the same – but the outcome is vastly different. After exactly the same amount of time and with the same interest rate, the only difference being he's now compounding his interest and principal, how much do you think cute little William finally accumulated for retirement?

The answer is quite astounding. At the end of 504 years of compounding the original penny at the same interest, William has $56,774,862,806 (that's 56 billion, 774 million, 862 thousand, 806 dollars!). That would fill one rather large money pouch!

Now realistically, none of us will live that long, but that won't matter – we should **all have more than one penny to invest at even higher rates of return** AND I'm sure <u>most of us will be happy with a few million</u>, rather than billion – don't you agree?

So – when it comes to investing and taking advantage of compounding, your very first step is to SAVE some money to invest. This is something you must start IMMEDIATELY. And if you're saying, "I don't have any money to put aside", read on – I'll help you find some!

 Wildly Wealthy Action Tip

Invest the money you've saved so it compounds and continues to multiply.

Little by Little
Start the Flow

As human beings, our greatness lies not so much in being able to remake the world... as in being able to remake ourselves.'
MAHATMA GANDHI

When I first decided to open what I called my "Financial Freedom Account", I had NO extra cash. I couldn't pay myself 10% of ANYTHING, but I really wanted to show the Universe I was serious about changing my financial situation. So I thought about what would be the easiest way for me to put some money aside – anything at all – and I decided **not to spend my coins**.

I made the decision that no matter what an item cost, I would only use paper money to pay for it. I would never spend coins again, and **all those coins I saved would be the start of my financial freedom**. I wanted to put them somewhere special, so I found myself two empty hot chocolate tins with plastic lids – one for silver coins and one for gold. I used monopoly money to decorate the tins, covered them in clear contact to stop the play money from falling off, put a slit in the top to drop the coins in, and so my saving plan began.

Every time I made a purchase, whether it cost 95c or 5c I NEVER used my coins. I only handed over notes. At the end of every day I put all my gold coins in one tin and all the silver and copper in another. **I was surprised at how easy it actually was, and how excited I became as those tins became heavier and heavier with my money**. At the end of the month I took my coins and nervously counted. I was amazed. After just one month I had $187 in coins to put into the bank. Let me tell you, I felt so incredibly proud of myself as I walked into the bank to deposit my coins. I had not had money in the bank, expressly for saving – EVER.

Occasionally, if I had been saving up for something in particular, I would put money aside (usually hidden in a cupboard) until I had enough to buy what I had my eye on. But my usual formula was to put it on credit and pay it back (or not, as the case often was). And here I was, at 39 years of age, putting money INTO THE BANK for the sole purpose of creating wealth, of investing, of becoming financially free. Now that was a BIG step.

You may find, as I did, that if you only have a set amount each month to spend, by making the decision not to spend your coins you don't actually seem to miss the money that you put aside. You seem to make choices based on what paper money is available. The money in those jars just seems to accumulate without you having to go without at all.

The other great thing about actually having money in the bank is it seems to **really shift your energy on a metaphysical level.** You KNOW you have money in the bank, no matter how small that amount may be. <u>Something happens to you inside when you have money put aside for the sole purpose of re-creating your financial future.</u> You become more attractive to money; you open yourself up to prosperity. You will find that abundance naturally begins to flow to you because, as you know, like attracts like, and that money in the bank wants some friends to play with; it wants you to attract more into your life. **Just do it and see what happens!**

 *Wildly Wealthy Action Tip*
Save your coins.

The Universe Abhors a Vacuum

'Out with the old, in with the new.'
ANON

Now the other way to find a little extra money and show the Universe just how committed you are, is to sell off things you have that you don't really need anymore.

If you're like most people, you probably have clothes hanging in your wardrobe that have been there for years waiting for you to lose those few kilos so you can fit back into them; or you've got boxes of children's toys that never get used; or maybe you've got kitchen appliances that have never been taken out of the box, or a garage full of items, and you don't even remember what's there – but you want to keep them, just in case you may want to use them again one day.

Often we're too scared to let go of the old, because we don't know when we will have the money to get the new or to get more. Well let me tell you a secret. The Universe abhors a vacuum. If you take the time to get rid of the old, it frees up energy; **it allows the Universe to bring more into your life, in all sorts of unexpected ways**.

The first thing you can do to make way for the new is have a garage or yard sale. Go through your house, room by room and cupboard by cupboard and take EVERYTHING you have not used, worn, played with or read for the last year and SELL IT. It doesn't matter how worn or old the item is, remember, **your trash is someone else's treasure**!

When you've had your sale – put ALL that money into your special savings account. That's right, it's not to go out and spend, it's to show the Universe you can do it! <u>You CAN save and you</u>

ARE serious about creating wealth in your life. You DO want to be rich. You ARE ready for prosperity. For even more money-magnetising energy, write those statements down in your Prosperity Binder – affirm it to the Universe! **When you set an intention, when you commit, the entire Universe conspires to make it happen!**

By selling off your excess items, you've achieved two steps in one – made space for the new AND you now have extra money to put into your special account!

OR, if you're really not into having a sale, you could donate to those less fortunate. Remember, for every item that you don't want or have sitting around not being used, there are probably thousands of people who would love to own or use it.

Moving house is a great time to put this into practice. Be ruthless and get your kids involved. I remember one time when I was making a very good income and living in a beautiful house on the water. Alas, I was still learning my lessons around money and the business I had created (selling personal development courses) came crashing down – there was a dispute with the printer that went on for almost nine months, during which time I didn't have a product to sell, and consequently NO INCOME. I had no

> *When you set an intention, when you commit, the entire Universe conspires to make it happen.*

choice but to move out of my beautiful house and rent something much cheaper in another area.

That Christmas things had been really tight and I remember looking at the few small presents scattered under the Christmas tree. I was giving my daughter hair clips (nothing fancy mind you, just those plain brown ones) and my son corn chips and salsa dip as presents – so we were really getting to the lowest of our low times.

As we were packing everything up, I said to my children, "**be ruthless; if you don't use it all the time, give it to the poor children**". Looking back, I realise at the time – they were the poor children! Yes, from the outside things looked fine. They went to a private school their Dad paid for and they lived in a nice home – but they went without on a daily basis, year after year. There were years when my children never asked me for a weekly video or an ice-cream or a packet of chips when we were out. They didn't ask if we could go to the movies, or buy their lunch at school – because they already knew what my answer would be. **It had to be no.** If I did happen to lash out and buy my kids lunch at school – I remember my son being so overjoyed, he would be jumping around with happiness and smothering me with kisses!

When it came to getting rid of the old to make way for the new – and I knew that was a strategy that worked –we were ruthless. I was too busy packing to think about selling anything, so I gave it all to a group called *Women helping Women*. We threw out everything that we didn't absolutely need and moved into our downgraded rental home. And sure enough, after months and months of no income whatsoever (except the sole parent benefit) the next week I made $9000, which seemed like a million dollars at the time. I was able to pay off a few old debts and keep us going for another month or so – **taking me step by step towards being a Wildly Wealthy Woman!**

I thoroughly recommend you take the time to de-clutter your home and get rid of all those things you don't use. And I don't just mean little things. You may have a jet ski, or boat, motorbike or caravan – something big that only gets used once a year. If you were to sell off that item, and invest the money, you could end up becoming totally financially free YEARS earlier and be able to purchase as many of those items as you want. You could be in a position to buy the latest and the greatest, even a new one each year, without it being any financial burden at all. You may have to **show the Universe just how committed you are** to creating long-term financial freedom, by shuffling things around in your life right now.

Also, apart from actually selling off all the big and little items around your home that you don't need or use, it is a really good idea to simply de-clutter your home. By that I mean, go through every room and throw out the rubbish that is hiding in cupboards, drawers, shelves and boxes.

Don't think you have to do this in one day (particularly if you seem to accumulate at the rate that I do!) Just choose one room, and in that one room choose one cupboard, and in that one cupboard choose one drawer, and then thoroughly clear out anything that is not required. And the next day, move onto the next drawer, and on and on until you have completed that cupboard, and so on until you have completed that room. Then move onto the next room until you have de-cluttered your entire house.

> *When you're in the flow, you begin to attract your desires to you much faster and with less effort!*

Mind you, you may get on a roll and find you spend an entire weekend sorting and filing and throwing out things, as it is such an energiser when it's all done. <u>This exercise alone will allow you to free up so much stagnant and wasted energy in your life and you will begin to feel more in the flow</u>, and when you're in the flow, everything seems effortless.

When you're in the flow, **you begin to attract your desires to you much faster and with less effort**. Start today!

 Wildly Wealthy Action Tips

Clear your clutter.

Sell off what you don't need or donate it to a worthwhile charity.

Poverty or Prosperity Consciousness?

'What we're after in prospering is nothing less
than a major shift in consciousness —
in the attitudes, beliefs and ideas you have about yourself
and your relationship to money.'
JERROLD MUNDIS

I noticed very clearly when I began to attract more money into my life, that I had trouble KEEPING it in my life. The more money I had flowing in, **the more unexpected bills and events I had occurring** that kept taking that money straight back out again.

I found 'money drainers' coming to me from all directions – far more than would normally come in for the same amount of time. The washing machine broke down, library books went missing, a tooth cracked in half and I needed a crown, videos were always late, I had a little accident in my car, the dishwasher kept jamming, the clothes dryer stopped heating, the stereo blew up and even the Department of Social Security (welfare dept) decided they'd overpaid me about five years earlier and I owed them around $7000! **As the flow coming in increased – it grew ever bigger going out!** So I was still broke.

Do you have that challenge when you seem to make more, but then you suddenly find more bills and debts mounting up? This is where your comfort zone comes into play. <u>This is where you need to stretch where you are financially (in your mind first) or you simply won't ever change your circumstances</u>. As you read through this book, you will find dozens of ways to stretch that financial comfort zone!

When I realised my money was flowing out just as fast as it was flowing in, even though I had far more than I'd ever had before, I began to study what makes people LOSE all that money after they win the lottery, and what makes Millionaires MAKE all that money after they go bankrupt. I wanted to know why some people attracted money easily, and some people worked hard but struggled financially all their life. Although it took a lot of time (and plenty of money – aahh, more debt!), I discovered some very interesting facts.

Your level of prosperity is determined by two things that you are probably blissfully unaware of! The first is whether you are programmed for poverty or prosperity, and the second is what your comfort zone around money currently is.

Now the first part, your prosperity or poverty consciousness around money, can be a little bit sneaky. Your mind or brain is a complex and wondrous tool but, like any tool, it can be used or misused. It's very much like a computer – it acts as a data storage and feedback device.

The problem is, on a conscious level you may desire money, love the idea of being rich and get excited about your financial freedom, but on a subconscious level, something is undermining your chance to live a life of richness – something you're probably unaware of.

Much of your data input began long before you had any say in what you wanted to believe. Through the teachings, casual comments and general conversation of your parents, friends, school, religion, community, media etc. data is stored in your mind. That data then becomes your own thoughts, opinions and beliefs, unless you make the conscious effort to change them.

For instance, how often did you hear some of the following statements when you were growing up, like I did, and how often do you hear those same words coming out of your own mouth?

◇ Money doesn't grow on trees (actually you CAN cultivate your own money tree and I'll give you some tips later)

◇ It takes money to make money (well, yes and no, a little money can get you started, but it doesn't have to be your OWN money – using OPM [other people's money] is the next level; find out more at www.WildlyWealthy.com)

◊ Money can't buy happiness (let me tell you from first hand experience, it's a heck of a lot more fun having money than NOT having money!)

◊ Money doesn't come easy (it can if you let it)

◊ You have to work hard for your money (not in this day and age)

◊ We can't afford it (it's better to think, 'How can we afford it?')

◊ Don't be greedy (there is NOTHING wrong with wanting more – the more you have, the more you can help yourself, family, friends and others)

◊ Filthy rich, stinking rich (I LOVE the scent of money!)

◊ How did they get so much money? They must be dealing drugs (there are thousands of ethical, legitimate ways to create wealth and I'll show you some)

◊ The rich get richer and the poor get poorer (can be the opposite if they begin thinking differently)

◊ Money is the root of all evil (it's actually 'the worship of money is the root of all evil', and I personally believe it's the lack of money which is the root of all evil)

What I found was, we travel through life having adopted OTHER people's beliefs and, as I said before, often don't even realise what our subconscious or 'default' is running on.

For instance, my family was not rich as I was growing up, but we were by no means poor either. We had to go without now and again but always seemed to have enough and lived quite comfortably. I would have thought I had a prosperity consciousness.

Now my mum and dad lived on a mountain – not an enormously big mountain, but a mountain none-the-less and they drove up and down that mountain every day. I remember my daughter coming home from their place a few years ago and telling me how it was really scary in the car with Nana and Pop because "When Pop gets to the top of the mountain, he turns the car off and rolls down the hill". And let me tell you, he's not doing that because he enjoys the thrill of not having total control; he's doing it to save money on petrol!

I'd totally forgotten my Dad did that, and it suddenly became clear to me; I realised that my family had a true poverty consciousness, and whether or not I was aware of it, it would be running in my subconscious too.

But wait…there's more! A few months ago I dropped my little Landrover Freelander into the service centre near my house, and because I needed to be somewhere by a certain time I asked my Dad if he could pick me up, which he happily did. As we were driving along we got to the traffic lights, which were red, and stopped. Guess what Dad did – he turned the engine OFF! And the worst part of all was, my parents had an absolute bomb of a car. The brakes were almost shot, you usually had to try at least two or three times before it would actually start, and as you were driving along, everything that could shake and rattle did!

> *This is why you want to be Wildly Wealthy – Because it's FUN.*

It was the sort of car where you couldn't be sure if the engine would ever start again. It wasn't the sort of car you wanted to be turning off in the middle of peak hour traffic – you could be stuck there for the next few hours!

Last year when Mum and Dad came over on Christmas Day, I made them find their present through a rhyming treasure hunt. They had to work out through each little rhyme where to find the next clue until finally it led them to their present. I designed the hunt so it took them into each room and past the presents the kids had received for Christmas so they could show off all their goodies! Mum and Dad followed the trail, and as they got near the end, they found some seat covers under the big palm tree out the front of our house. When they were opening that present my daughter gave them one last rhyme that said something like, "Oh yes of course, it is so true, look around for the colour blue" (I'm not a poet as you can see). Then I handed them a set of car keys tied with a big red ribbon.

Mum looked at the keys and thought I wanted her to get something blue out of the boot of my car. We prompted them to 'look around' and as Mum and Dad both looked around, it took a couple of moments for it to actually sink in that these were the keys to their new blue car which I'd parked across the road. And when it did, believe me, I thought my mum was going to pass out – she couldn't breathe and started sobbing uncontrollably. And Dad, who does NOT cry, even had to wipe his eyes.

Mum and Dad were the talk of their retirement resort. They said it was "Like we'd won the lottery". Word spread like wildfire and **they had people coming to congratulate them and take a peek at their new car for the next month!**

<u>This is why you want to be RICH</u>; this is why you want to create financial freedom; this is why you want to be Wildly Wealthy – <u>because it's FUN!</u>

 Wildly Wealthy Action Tip

Take a moment to think about your upbringing with money and the words you heard as you were growing up.

Recognize a poverty default? Well you're in the right place. By the end of this book **you <u>will</u> have a Prosperity Consciousness.**

Will the Universe Make YOU Rich?

'How rich can you be?
As rich as you think you can be, or as wealthy as your contentment
level.
However most people are content in just 'getting by' and if that is as
far as your consciousness can expand, then so be it.
You have made that choice.
But know that you can achieve the total freedom of
financial independence if you choose.'

JOHN RANDOLPH PRICE

As I've already stated, **quantum physics has proven that everything in our world is vibrating** – everything – including our thoughts. And you attract to yourself whatever you give your attention and energy to – whether wanted or unwanted. This Law of Attraction is like gravity – we can't put it in a petrie dish and show it to you. It's a bit like radio waves – you can't see them, but you know for sure they are working. The Law of Attraction is the same – **you can't see it, but it's working all the time.**

You have a choice as to where your energy or attention is focussed. As Napoleon Hill says in the classic *Think and Grow Rich* – "You will know that we are drawn, almost like a magnetic force toward that which we focus on". You can choose to focus on what is working in your life and what you want more of, or you can choose to focus on what isn't working and what you don't want. **Either way you get more of whatever it is you focus on.**

I am totally in love with The Metaphysical. I love that we can create our own world simply by our thoughts and I love to share everything I know with anyone who will listen – including my children. I mean, why wouldn't you want your children to get a handle on this wonderful information now, rather than in another 20 or 30 years?

I'm continually telling my kids, "What you focus on is what becomes your reality." When I was in my stage of attracting money but it was flowing out just as fast, my daughter would say, **"blah blah blah. We don't need a lecture about that spiritual stuff, it doesn't work anyway – we've still got no money".**

And that was the truth; we were still struggling financially even though I was saying my affirmations and visualizing what I desired a couple of times a day. But the problem was, the rest of time I was seeing bills and feeling my solar plexus tighten; I was experiencing fear, worry and panic about where the money would come from, that I would never have enough, that I would be struggling forever.

I had to stop and look at what I was creating for myself when my daughter was around twelve and wanted to go to her school dance.

She takes after me (a bit disorganised and leaves things to the last minute!) and she came to me on the Thursday – with the dance being the next day – and said, "Mum, I need some new shorts for the dance".

> *You can choose to focus on what is working in your life and what you want more of, or you can choose to focus on what isn't working and what you don't want. Either way you get more of whatever it is you focus on.*

Now I need you to really get this picture – **I was having a really, really tragic week financially.** At that stage I wasn't tracking my finances; I'd had a cheque bounce, a few bills had come in, including a red-letter bill (those scary ones), and I was beginning to go into my usual panic mode around money.

So the conversation went a little like this…"Can you buy me my shorts and shoes, I really need them?" "Darling, I don't have the money right now". "You never buy me anything; I have to have them!" "Darling, I said I don't have the money". "Can't you just put it on your credit card?"

Now, the credit card was up to the limit, so that wasn't an option. And by this time I'm **starting to freak out**. I am seething with all sorts of very negative, very strong emotions. **Frustration**, because even though I was making good money, it was disappearing; **embarrassment**, because I felt so hopeless at managing my money; **guilt**, because I felt like a bad mother for not being able to buy things for her; **sadness**, because I knew how disappointed she would be because she'd be missing out once again and **anger**, because she was asking me for something I just didn't have. <u>Unfortunately, anger was winning, and the picture was not pretty</u>…

> *By changing your thoughts it's possible to begin attracting mountains of money, riches, wealth and prosperity into your life.*

The veins on my temples were throbbing, my eyes were bulging out of their sockets, I was hissing through gritted teeth, I had spit flying out of my mouth and I'm sure there were traces of steam coming out of my ears as **I screamed like a banshee going to war** "I don't have the money to pay all our bills, I've got to try and pay the phone bill before they cut it off. We just don't have the money – don't you understand; we're broke right now – WE DON'T HAVE ANY MONEY!!!!!!"

Then she looked me squarely in the eye and in all the wisdom of her twelve years upon this earth, (and many lifetimes before) said to me in her **most disgusted tone**, "<u>Well if that's how you FEEL whenever you think about money – the Universe is NEVER going to make us rich.</u>"

And I felt like someone had just punched me in the stomach. In that moment, plain as day, I could see why I was still struggling financially. I was attaching my strongest emotions – all negative – to the one thing I wanted most. And in doing so, I was repelling it. I was pushing money away. I was making sure it didn't stay long enough for me to enjoy.

My emotional outburst was not about having money; it was about NOT having money. So 'not having money' was the dominant vibration or energy (or order) that I was sending out to the Universe day after day. And the Universe was picking up that 'not having money' order and giving it straight back to me, day after day. **So if you're not where you want to be financially, you may be doing the same thing – repelling abundance, prosperity and total financial freedom, by your thoughts**.

But the exciting thing is, **by changing your thoughts** (using the many ideas in this book) **it's possible to begin attracting <u>mountains of money, riches, wealth and prosperity into your life, starting immediately</u>**.

Let's hope you're lucky enough to have someone close to you who can show you where your thoughts are around money – and I thought she didn't listen to a word I said!

 Wildly Wealthy Action Tip

Focus your strongest emotions on how much money you DO have and believe you can have, and feel wonderful about having it.

Predominant
Mental Attitude

'Our best friends and our worst enemies are our thoughts.
A thought can do us more good than a doctor
or banker or a faithful friend.
It can also do us more harm than a brick.'

DR. FRANK CRANE

It's quite simple really – **we attract into our life everything we desire through our thoughts and the power of our mind**. We attract abundance, prosperity and riches into our lives when we attach emotions such as love, desire and gratitude for the money (no matter how little) we do have in our life. And we repel abundance, prosperity and riches just as easily, by attaching fear, frustration and anger to our thoughts around the lack of money in our lives.

Maybe you are already doing some great 'attracting work' around money. You could be visualizing yourself as wealthy, doing chosen affirmations around abundance, reading your goals on creating riches and generally putting it 'out there'. But on average, you think around 60,000 thoughts a day and 90% of these are repetitive. **Many of them are the same (poverty consciousness) thoughts you had this morning, last night, last week, last month, last year** – is it any wonder you stay in the same place financially year after year?

So I decided, after being clearly shown that my default thoughts were focusing on lack, I would begin to consciously focus on abundance. The interesting thing is you don't have to focus on riches and wealth 24 hours a day 7 days a week, to attract more of it into your life. <u>Wealth just has to be your predominant mental attitude or focus.</u> In other words, **you just have to be** focusing more on abundance than on the lack of abundance to begin to bring it into your experience.

For instance, lets say you are doing a half-hour meditation morning and night, visualising three times a day and reading out your goals or affirmations three times day – you still have around fourteen hours (if you take out your sleeping time) when you do what I call 'unconscious affirmations' – when you continually think the same things over and over again. Those 'unconscious affirmations' are the ones that continue to sabotage all the good work you are doing. So all you need to do is make a shift in your focus toward prosperity and abundance to create wealth beyond your wildest dreams – **I'm telling you, it's that easy.** Simply shutting out the media, consistently doing your Abundance Breaths and being grateful on a daily basis may be big enough changes for your entire predominant mental attitude to shift.

Because predominant doesn't mean every second, it means 'the most'. For instance if you're thinking about bills, debts and how little you have 49% of the time, and then focusing on prosperity and abundance 51% of the time – your predominant mental attitude would be toward creating wealth. Now, let me just add if that WAS the case, it would probably be a slow and arduous journey with money continually coming in and going out and coming in and going out and you'd never quite seem to get too far ahead. With a percentage breakdown like that, **it's a little like trying to drive a car with one foot on the accelerator and one foot on the brake.** <u>You will be hopping erratically and not really getting anywhere FAST!</u>

It's exactly the same with your predominant mental attitude. As long as you **MAINLY think about what you DO want to attract into your life, then it is sure to come; it HAS to happen.** But your results will be so much quicker and appear so much easier if you focus on what you want 70% of time, or 80%, or maybe even 90%.

 Wildly Wealthy Action Tip

Be aware of your thoughts – focus on HAVING money.

Millionaire Plan

'Have in your mind that which would constitute a miracle for you.
Get the vision. Suspend disbelief and scepticism.
Allow yourself to take the journey toward real magic.'
DR. WAYNE DYER

After my conversation (or should I say ugly outburst) with my daughter, I realised I had to do something to change my focus; I took action. I decided to write an affirmation that I could run over and over in my mind so I didn't have time to think any negative thoughts around money.

Affirmations are deliberately and concisely constructed statements (often silent) which, when properly understood, and applied, will totally transform your future.

The use of affirmations is often misunderstood and frequently seen as metaphysical nonsense. You may have tried using affirmations at some time and are now thinking, "They don't work; they're a waste of time" and let me tell you, **you're absolutely right – unless you use them properly**! Affirmations are nothing more than a string of words which won't do anything or make any difference in your life **UNLESS you know how to use them for maximum effectiveness.** Similar to an aeroplane being nothing more than a big piece of steel sitting on the runway, which won't do anything unless you know how to use it. When you get that plane's engine revved up, and you give it fuel, and you give it power, it takes off and goes out into the Universe and will take you wherever you want to go. <u>When you give your affirmations fuel and energy and power, they too will take off, go out into the Universe and attract back to you all the prosperity and riches you desire.</u>

You HAVE to give them power to get your results, and there are two ways to do this: with repetition and with emotion.

You're already using affirmations, although maybe in a negative way:

◊ I'm hopeless at maths

◊ I am so fat

◊ I'll never be able to afford it

◊ I'm always late

◊ I never have any luck

The use of positive affirmations will change your life for the better, as I will confirm. So after the scene with my daughter, I decided to change my subconscious programming by saying, "I am a debt-free millionaire" because I thought that would be a pretty cool thing to be. But the minute those words left my lips, my mind screamed, "Liar, Liar pants on fire, you are no such thing; what a load of rubbish; who are you kidding? You're broke!" Well, the first thing you have to know about affirmations is, for them to work, you have to BELIEVE the words you're saying.

> *When you give your affirmations fuel and energy and power, they too will attract back to you all the prosperity and riches you desire!*

As the Bible says:

'Whatsoever thing ye desire, when ye pray,
believe that ye have received it, and it will be yours.'

Affirm is the metaphysical term for Pray, so in other words, "If you believe your desire has already come to you, **it has to appear**". So I decided to put in some qualifiers, or take 'baby steps' as I call them, to help me to believe what I was saying.

I started by affirming, "I am now ready to accept that I am now in the process of becoming a debt-free millionaire". Although that was a mouthful, I could totally believe that I was **ready to accept** that I was **in the process** and I was **becoming** a debt-free millionaire. So I said my new affirmation morning, noon and night. I said it when I was in the shower, when I was driving the kids to school, when I was hanging out washing, when I was cleaning the house and when I went to sleep. If I didn't have to consciously think of anything else, I would be saying my affirmation over and over in my mind. I said it so often, that if I woke in the middle of the night it was running through my head. That's when I KNEW that I was beginning to change the default from poverty consciousness to prosperity consciousness.

After a couple of days, I dropped some of the baby steps and said, "I am now in the process of becoming a debt free millionaire". Then after a couple of days of feeling really comfortable saying that, I changed it to, "I am now becoming a debt free millionaire" and then finally, **"I am now a debt free millionaire"**. The process took around a week to go from my first very long-winded affirmation to my final, ideal affirmation. As I mentioned, I said this morning noon and night, and those few words seemed to shift everything. Understand, that before I began this process, my continual negative subconscious thinking was sabotaging all the good I was doing with meditations and visualizations, but once I changed my 'default' to focus on what I DID want, the outside picture changed as well.

So the sequence for my successful affirmation was:

◇ **I am now** ready to accept that I am now in the process of becoming **a debt-free millionaire**

◇ **I am now** in the process of becoming **a debt-free millionaire**

◇ **I am now** becoming **a debt-free millionaire**

◇ **I am now a debt-free millionaire**

And the great thing was, a month after I began my consistent around the clock affirmation, I had the best month ever in my new personal development business. I made $46,000 profit in that month alone; that's more than I had made for the previous 3 years – combined.

I was on my way to being Wildly Wealthy!

 Wildly Wealthy Action Tips

Become aware of the negative affirmations you are running through your mind and replace them with positive ones.

Use the four-part 'baby-steps' process outlined previously, to create your own positive affirmation and repeat often.

Go to www.WildlyWealthy.com for a list of Affirmations for Abundance to assist you to create your OWN powerful affirmations

Affirm Your Desires

'All that we are is the result of all that we have thought.
It is founded on thought.
It is based on thought.'
BUDDHA

The secret to getting results is choosing an affirmation that is right for you. Here are some tips for getting the most out of your affirmations:

1. Write them down

2. Make them **short and to the point**

3. Make your affirmations appropriate – you want to use words that detail your goals **as if the end result has already occurred**.

4. State them in the present, such as "I now" or "I am" – this 'tricks' your subconscious into thinking it has already happened, thereby making you more aware of circumstances, events or people who WILL make your stated affirmation a reality. Say them **as if they have already happened**.

5. Always make your affirmations positive such as "I am", "I do", "I can", "I always", or "I now" rather than "I don't want to crave chocolate," as your subconscious drops the negative word and focuses on the rest – in this case you will continue to crave chocolate! It would be much better to say, "I now choose to eat only healthy, life-giving foods". **Only state what you want, never what you don't want.**

6. Make them **personal** and in the first person. Always say "I" and feel the sense of responsibility when you say your affirmations.

7. Place them on a mirror or wall where you will **see them often.**

8. **Say them out loud** as often as you can.

9. Mix strong, powerful and positive emotions with your affirmations. Feel the joy of achievement and success as you repeat them to yourself. **Emotion adds amazing power** to your affirmations.

10. Add the **power of visualization**. Close your eyes and see the end result as having been achieved; feel how good that feels and know that you CAN achieve anything your heart desires through your words, your actions and the power of your mind!

11. Say them over and over and over again. **Repetition is the key** to implanting your affirmations firmly in the subconscious from where you will then draw your desire into your life.

Whatever you decide to affirm, you must be able to make yourself believe it on some level. If you are bringing in $2000 a month, don't jump to affirming you make $20,000 a month if you feel it is absolutely not possible. Start by affirming, "I now make $4000 a month", and then when you totally believe that with your heart and soul, you can raise the bar – increase the amount and continue to do so until you get to your ideal income. **Keep in mind, you want to stretch, not snap!**

When your desires and your imagination are in conflict, your imagination invariably wins.

Some affirmations you may like to use:

◇ Money and success flow to me in avalanches of abundance

◇ I am open to receive even more money and success

◇ Rivers of prosperity and abundance flow to me

◇ Every day I am getting richer and richer

◇ I create money and abundance day and night

◊ I am swimming in a sea of abundance

◊ I deserve abundance and prosperity

◊ I am a money magnet, money is drawn to me from everywhere

◊ I am rich, abundant and wealthy

◊ I am wildly wealthy

◊ I am increasingly magnetic to money, abundance and prosperity

It's most important to remember: "When your desires and your imagination are in conflict, your imagination invariably wins." In other words, you can't hold two contradictory ideas in your mind at the same time. Your mind will attempt to harmonise the inner conflict in two ways: it will replace the old idea and accept the new idea through repetition, affirmations and visualisations; or it will use the existing idea, which is your 'comfort zone', and totally reject the new idea.

Your subconscious will always accept the stronger of the two opposing ideas. In other words, if you make the following statements, you're doomed to failure.

"I want to be wealthy, but I'm hopeless with money"

"I want to start a new business, but I'm too busy"

"I want a relationship, but I'm not good enough"

"I want to lose weight, but I'm always hungry"

"I want to be rich, because I'm always broke"

What you are doing is attempting to impress two opposing ideas into your subconscious, and the strongest (most deeply ingrained in your subconscious) is usually the negative, or you wouldn't have instantly thought it. You'll then get the opposite of what you desire. If you are ready to live the life of your dreams, you must harmonise your desire and imagination – you must get rid of the conflict. You do that by affirming ONLY what you want, not what is, or what you don't want – **only what you DO want!** When there's no longer a quarrel between your conscious and subconscious minds your desire will appear. It has to, there is no question.

Another great idea is to record your affirmations onto a CD or tape and play them softly in the background as you go about your day's work. Play them as you are gently drifting off to sleep. You might prefer to record them on an 'endless loop' tape that just continues to go round and round playing the same affirmations over and over. This is a powerful way to deeply ingrain your desires into your subconscious. Be careful that you only make your recording when you are feeling 'vibrationally high' as your energy as well as your words will be absorbed each time you listen. www.WildlyWealthy.com has a list of recommended Prosperity and subliminal recordings if you would prefer a ready-made audio.

Above all, don't let your logical mind kick in and tell you it's not possible. Remember your warehouse with your name on it? **You only have that desire because it's there waiting to be delivered!**

 Wildly Wealthy Action Tips

Create a new affirmation for yourself and begin to repeat it consistently.

Visit www.WildlyWealthy.com for a list of affirmations you can use, or pre-recorded affirmations to listen to.

Double Your Attraction Powers

'You can have anything you want…
You must want it with an exuberance that erupts through the skin
and joins the energy that created the world'
SHEILA GRAHAM

Since my first success with constant repetition of affirmations I have learnt to use an even more powerful method and that is, repeating AND **attaching strong emotion**.

The way an affirmation works is through the subconscious. There are two ways a belief gets lodged in your subconscious and they are: through repetition or through strong emotion. Remember when you learnt the times tables at school – you can probably say them easily now without even thinking. They're lodged in your subconscious, and the way they got there was through repetition; over and over until they became a 'knowing' – **you don't have to think about them on a conscious level**.

To give you another example, you might have a toddler in the kitchen, and you could say to that child, "Stay away from the stove or you'll burn yourself" and every time they go near the stove you say the same thing again, "Stay away from the stove or you'll burn yourself". You could say it 20 times and that child may still try and touch the stove, but eventually the words will sink in and she will stay away.

Just imagine for a moment that you say those same words, but the child ignores you and goes straight to the stove, touches it with her hand and gets burnt. Let me tell you right now, you will never have to say those words to that child again, because the surge of emotion (in this case fear) that she felt in that moment, has made that a 'knowing' for her; it has gone directly to her subconscious mind. That child will never go near that hot stove again!

It's the same with attracting what you desire with affirmations. To get the result you want, **the affirmation has to go into your subconscious and become a knowing**.

You can either do that through constant repetition, which can take time, OR you can attach strong emotion to the affirmation and it will go directly into the subconscious where it goes into action to make you more magnetic to your desires. Both methods work, but when you use repetition WITH emotion, the attraction powers double!

> *This is a powerful way to give your affirmations the energy required to attract back to you your desires of abundance, riches and wealth.*

So, create your own affirmation using the 'baby-steps' method as before, you can say it over and over and over and get the result you want Or you could add emotion OR you could **combine the two** as I did...

I had another affirmation that I really liked:

"I am so grateful that I now make at least $10,000 profit every month."

I used very specific words, because I didn't want to limit myself to a certain amount if I could make more (*at least*); I also didn't want to make a lot of money and then have a lot of expenses (*profit*); and I didn't want it to be a one-time thing, so I made sure I could get consistent results (*every month*).

That affirmation used all the criteria: it was in the present; it was personal; it had emotion; it was powerful – and it had the end result clearly defined.

When I said that affirmation I really put a lot of emotion into it. I repeated it slowly sixteen times (that's how many words there are when you say each word) and each time I emphasized a different word.

For instance, the first time I emphasized the first word…

"**I** am so grateful that I now make at least $10,000 profit every month"

The second time, the second word…

"I **am** so grateful that I now make at least $10,000 profit every month"

The third time, the third word…

"I am **so** grateful that I now make at least $10,000 profit every month"

…and on I went.

Each time you should really feel the emphasized word in your heart and soul. Flood your body with the emotions you would feel if your affirmation had already come to be. Again, close your eyes as you repeat your affirmation and see it as already having happened.

This is a powerful way to give your affirmations the energy required to send them out into the Universe and speedily attract back to you your desires of abundance, riches and wealth!

At the time, $10,000 each and every month seemed like a fortune. At the time it seemed like quite a stretch – although I knew I could do it because I had 'fluked' a $46,000 profit in one month. Now, I can make that in a week, and sometimes in a day. I'm telling you; this stuff really works! If I was able to change my financial situation with the poverty consciousness that I had running through my head – YOU WILL TOO!

 Wildly Wealthy Action Tip

Add strong emotion to give your affirmations even more life and power.

Discover Your Hidden Dollars

'Too many people spend money they haven't earned,
to buy things they don't want,
to impress people they don't know'
WILL ROGERS

Never were truer words spoken. In today's society, people seem to think that they should have EVERYTHING they want, and immediately. Now there's nothing wrong with having it all, but using the power of the plastic (credit card) to manifest, rather than the power of your mind, will only get you into more money trouble.

Robert Kiyosaki (author of the Rich Dad, Poor Dad series of books) states *"It is well known that Millionaires spend money on things that grow in value, while the poor spend money on things that lose value."* **You must make your money work for you, instead of you working for your money.**

Because my parents were so 'careful' with their money, I made the decision (not on a conscious level) that I was NOT going to be like them.

I would buy what I wanted, when I wanted. I was different. I was blessed. I made myself believe I always seemed to get what I wanted (all the while going deeper and deeper into debt). Although I hated the way my parents always seemed to be scrimping and saving, I have to admit, that once I decided to be responsible with my money – to show the Universe that I could be entrusted with more – the lessons I learnt from my parents on how to do more with less were invaluable.

Now I am a big advocate of being frugal. And just so you're aware, being frugal is NOT the same as being a penny-pinching miser like Scrooge McDuck. It's about being careful and making sensible choices when it comes to spending.

In the book *The Millionaire Next Door* Thomas Stanley and William Danko dispel the myth that Millionaires drive around in flashy cars, own mansions with yachts moored on their jetties, are dripping with jewellery and throw $100 notes around like they're petty cash. In fact, they say the majority of Millionaires are careful with their money - buying used cars, repairing their shoes, opting for lower priced clothing and living in normal homes in average neighbourhoods.

Most Millionaires became Millionaires by being Frugal until their investments began producing enough additional income for them to either spend as they wish, or be in the position of never having to work again (some continue to be frightfully frugal even when they have more than they could ever spend – but that's another story!)

So just what is Frugal? Well, the dictionary definition is as follows:

Frugal – economical in use or expenditure: prudently saving or sparing

Economical – avoiding waste or extravagance

Prudent – wisely cautious – careful of one's own interests – careful in providing for the future

The idea of being frugal and saving money with each purchase, is not to then spend it on the latest MP3 player or hipster jeans, it's to pay off your debts faster, and then invest so that you become financially free.

The **spirit with which you undertake saving this money is vital** – if you do it from a place of lack, you will attract more lack, but if you do it from a place of excitement about paying off debts faster and having more to invest, you will attract more money.

If you implement even half of these strategies – you will save thousands of dollars a year and can then make better choices as to where that money goes (pay off debts or invest to multiply). You may find it helpful to put the money saved **immediately** into your savings account, or use it to **pay off a bill that very same day**, otherwise it will often evaporate into other expenses.

Don't look at each small amount saved as not really worthwhile. It all adds up. That seemingly small amount you save each day, each week, each month and ultimately each year, will make an enormous difference when it comes to paying off your debts, and will continue to grow and multiply when invested.

Use some of the following ideas to help YOU find more money (the approximate frequency and money saved are in brackets):

◊ Only use your own bank's ATM – You pay between $2-$4 each time you use another bank's ATM ($4 x 52 = $208pa)

◊ **Don't buy take-away food, or buy less (1 per week $25 x 52 = $1300pa)**

◊ Take your lunch ($10 per day $50 x 52 = $2600pa)

◊ **Take morning/afternoon** tea ($8 per day $40 x 52 = $2080pa)

◊ Make the kids' lunch (2 children x 2 @ $5 = $20 = $700pa)

◊ **Buy generic brands eg. Toilet paper, baked beans, rice, porridge/rolled oats (save $520 pa)**

◊ Stop renting videos – tape good shows on TV (1 video per week $7 x 52 = $364pa)

◊ **Comparison shop – buy things on special – particularly food items. ($20 per week = $1000pa)**

◊ Limit your newspaper/magazine subscriptions – read friends' (2 magazines and 7 newspapers approx. $10.95 x 52 = $569pa)

◊ **Do phone-rate check-ups – use a phone card for international calls (save $1500pa)**

◊ Don't buy books – go to library or learn from free teleclasses (at least 2 books/tapes sets a month $2000pa)

◊ **Stop spending coins ($200 per month save $2400pa)**

◇ Shop once a week, not every time you need something.

◇ **Don't pay to go to more seminars/training classes/ teleclasses etc – implement everything you know before you spend more**

◇ Barter your services or products

◇ **Cancel cable TV ($54.90 per month save $659pa)**

◇ Don't buy soft drinks – water is cheaper and healthier ($17.50 x 52 = $910pa)

◇ **Stop smoking ($9 x 7 = $63 x 52 = $3276pa)**

◇ Buy scratched or dented whitegoods (they usually get damaged during delivery anyway!)

◇ **Would you go and rip up $5 notes each week and throw them in the bin? That's what you do with food that goes uneaten and rotten or fruit that gets overripe before you eat it. Only buy as much fresh fruit and vegetables as you need for that week.**

◇ Pay bills regularly – don't pay late /disconnection fees

◇ **Don't let cheques bounce – (around $40 per cheque)**

If you like these ideas, read the Wildly Wealthy Action Tip at the end of this chapter to discover how you can receive a complete e-book with more great ways to save money.

If you feel WONDERFUL about saving money to pay off debts or invest, then the energy you create will attract more money!

Remember, it is the spirit with which you implement your money-saving tips that will either STOP the flow of prosperity or OPEN the flow to you. If you feel you are hard-done-by, if you feel you are missing out, **if you focus on the lack – you will stop the flow in**. Whereas, <u>if you feel WONDERFUL about saving money to pay off</u>

debts or invest, then the energy you create will attract more money. That is the desired outcome.

I remember talking about how to create your Millionaire Mindset at a wealth creation seminar where a multi-millionaire was also speaking. During one of the lunch breaks he wanted to know more about what I taught, so I shared some of the more practical strategies (I thought my metaphysical tips might be too much for him!).

He was particularly excited about being frugal and wanted to share some of his own ideas. Remember I said before that there's a difference between frugal and stingy, well, I think he and his wife had just tipped the scales in the wrong direction! When he shared the next tip I thought he was joking... His wife makes his lunch and wraps it in cling wrap (that sticky plastic wrap) to keep it fresh. She then makes him bring it home to be washed and used for the next day's lunch. Is that going too far? Who knows, obviously not for them, because **it's all about how you FEEL when you are frugal**. If you feel like **you are saving money and are excited about it**, <u>you will attract more money</u>, if you feel you are going without, you will attract more of 'going without'.

So have FUN saving money and you will see more of it in your life.

 Wildly Wealthy Action Tips

Enjoy being frugal.

Put the money you've saved directly into your savings/ investment account or pay off debts.

Visit <u>www.WildlyWealthy.com</u> to get your Hidden Treasure e-book with over 101 great ways to find more money to set you financially free.

Open the
Abundance Flow

'Affluence is the experience in which our needs are easily met and our desires spontaneously fulfilled.'
DEEPAK CHOPRA

I'll bet if I were to ask which you enjoy the most, money coming in, or money going out, I'd already know the answer.

Honestly, how do you feel when it's time to gather together all your outstanding debts and bills, grab your cheque book and do what, for most people, is the end of month juggling trick (when there's more month than money)? I used to detest this time; it was not a joyful, fun-filled, exciting process. I was usually filled with **annoyance, anxiety, frustration and quite often, worry and fear**.

Did I have enough in my account to pay these bills? Would I still have money coming in the following weeks? What if I pay them all now and don't make any money for a while? Would I be better to not pay them and wait for the red letter? (I've had a LOT of them in the past!) Even if I had enough money in my account I still did not get excited. I would have **preferred the money stayed in my pocket** rather than going into theirs!

If you feel any of these emotions as you pay for things – <u>your focus is on the LACK of money</u> – and those **strong emotions are attracting exactly what you are focusing on — more lack**!

Here is the secret! You can begin to attract more money, simply by **enjoying paying your bills and delighting in circulating your money**. Sound a little crazy? But it's true! By changing your energy, your focus and the emotions **attached to the money flowing out**, <u>you will see more flowing in</u>!

The fact of the matter is, too many people LOVE money flowing in but HATE money flowing out and then wonder why that flow seems a little (or a lot) blocked. **Money is filled with the very same energy and intelligence that flows through the entire Universe, from which it was created.** Money reacts to your attitudes about it. <u>Think favourably about money, both the flow in as well as the flow out, and you will multiply and increase it in your life</u>. Following is a simple exercise that can have a dramatic effect on the flow of money you see in your life!

"Think favourably about money, both the flow in as well as the flow out, and you will multiply and increase it in your life."

When it's time for you to pay your bills, take a moment to 'set the scene'. Create an atmosphere of peace and joy. For you that may mean lighting a candle, or burning some essential oils, or putting on some soothing background music. To begin to **love the experience of the flow out** as much as the flow in, there are two things you need to do from now on when you pay for anything.

The first is to be grateful – truly grateful. For instance if you are paying your electricity bill, rather than moan and groan about how your daughter had the air conditioner in her room cranked up all summer and your bill is now $200 more than usual, think of all the wonderful things that occurred in your life to generate that bill.

Feel how thankful you are that you are able to show the electricity company your gratitude for being able to use their service all summer.

In my case, I think about how I can dive in my beautiful clean swimming pool – kept that way by the electricity that runs the automatic cleaner. I can go to the fridge whenever I want to get a lovely cool drink, and then sit under the fan on a long hot summer's day. I love being able to listen to my favourite music when I feel like it, or read a book at the flick of a switch after the sun's gone down. I can connect to the world through my laptop, or cook up my yummiest dish when I'm hungry.

I am so grateful I can now send them money in appreciation for all the good I received from using that electricity, and the money I am paying really isn't enough to adequately show them how thankful I truly am.

And secondly, in addition to the thoughts of appreciation I send out, on the back of each cheque I write *thank you* or the words *prosperity* or *abundance*, or draw a big heart wrapped around a dollar sign in bright fluorescent markers. (I'm sure my bank manager thinks I'm crazy!)

The idea is to think about all the good you received from that service (electricity/phone/something you bought) and **now you're able to show how much you really appreciate them by sending money in return**. This exercise quickly changes how you feel about the flow going out!

That's what you're aiming for; to think and feel differently about money; to **feel joy and think only loving thoughts when you think about money**, both the money coming in and the money going out – and then you will begin to draw more of it to you.

You can also use a similar technique when you purchase something at the supermarket or shop. As you pass your money over to the shop assistant say, "Thank you so much for allowing me to pay for this product/service. I really appreciate it. Thank you." Of course, you don't have to say this out loud if you feel uncomfortable (gosh, I don't always verbalise my gratitude in that way); just smiling and saying thank-you while thinking thoughts of gratitude **will be enough to make you more magnetic to prosperity and abundance.**

Free up the energy you hold around money. Love it flowing in! Love it flowing out. Just love it, love it, love it – **you will see more of it in your life**!

 Wildly Wealthy Action Tips

Love the flow of money in.

Love the flow of money out.

Bless your money as it flows out.

Decorate your cheques.

I Love Money!

'Whatever may be said in praise of poverty,
the fact remains that it is not possible to live a really complete
or successful life unless one is rich.
You cannot rise to your greatest possible height in talent
or soul development unless you have plenty of money.'

WALLACE D. WATTLES

Are you ready to attract more money, wealth, riches and prosperity into your life? Then don't be shy about it, let the Universe hear your desire. Thinking and focusing on prosperity will draw it to you, but why not attach wings to your wishes – really put it out there! You know how much you want to spend time with people who love you! Money is the same – it will stay longer with people who **love it and respect it and look after it**.

When you jump out of bed every morning, go outside (as long as you don't mind your neighbours listening in if you're close) and chant to the dawn's new sky: "I love Money and Money loves me, I love Money and Money loves me, I love Money and Money loves me". Say this three times – three is a good power number,

> *Feel how much you LOVE money, feel how GOOD it feels to be abundant and prosperous!*

say it with meaning; **put your heartfelt emotions into it**. Say it in your mind over and over. Feel how much you LOVE money, feel how GOOD it feels to be abundant and prosperous.

To live the best life you can live, to develop yourself to your greatest heights, to be the best you can be and then be in a position to give more of yourself both personally and financially, **you must become Rich**. If, whenever you think of money, you are filled with emotions of worry and fear (because you are focusing on the LACK of money in your life), change that focus and instead, <u>fill your heart with love.</u> Perceive money as a loving energy that you are at one with. **Feel deserving of more love and money in your life and feel full of love for the money you do have.**

<u>Fill your heart with love; feel how wonderful that feels to be flooded with love in the form of abundance.</u> Be open to receiving even more love in the form of prosperity and money right now! Be open to allowing that flood of love and abundance into your life. Be open to allowing that flood of money into your life! Know that you are a unique, special, wonderful individual and the very fact that you are here on planet earth means **you are something special** and are here for a reason – even if it's not clear to you yet.

> *Keep your focus on what you **do** want – on prosperity and a life filled with riches and love.*

I learnt a wonderful and easy tip to keep focused on attracting ever-increasing Abundance into my life, which I used for years. I photocopied a couple of $100 notes (which as I've already said, is NOT to be attempted at home – although I am sure you can find some exceptionally realistic notes on the internet which you could print off for the same purpose.) I then put the $100 notes where I could see them all the time. One was stuck to my computer and one was behind the sun visor of my car.

If I was working or checking e-mails I would see that money. And every time I folded the sun visor down (which was pretty much every time I got in the car) I'd see that $100 note. I would pull the note out, chant "I love Money and Money loves me – and Money is drawn to me, just like a magnet", I used to then kiss it, and put it back in the visor. In fact, that note is still there, and I still kiss it now and again – I really do love Money, and I know that Money really does love me!

Again, this is a very simple but powerful tip to keep your focus on what you do want – **on prosperity and a life filled with riches and love.** Your aim is to have a pure and loving relationship with money – not that dysfunctional relationship you used to have. Don't just say the words with a hollow heart. Money prefers to spend time with people who respect, cherish and love it, so the more you learn to feel love, **not just think love but feel it deep within your heart**, the more magnetic to money you will be. In fact, not just money, you will become a magnet attracting all good things.

Wildly Wealthy Action Tip

Love your money and it will spend more time with you.

Go to www.WildlyWealthy.com to get your Wildly Wealthy FAST Companion Workbook with an additional I LOVE MONEY exercise.

Embrace Financial Freedom

'Live beneath your means —
don't make the mistake of looking good and going no-where.'
ROBERT KIYOSAKI

When you are in debt, when you are struggling to pay your bills each month, you have an enormous amount of energy around money – and it's usually all negative. It's almost as if you have this force field around you, and even if you are practising all these wonderful metaphysical techniques to attract money, it sometimes seems that your force field is so dense that **money has a lot of trouble actually appearing in your world**. So now is a good time to focus on getting out of debt.

Debt is actually an illusion that you have more money - it's really another form of poverty. When you put something on a credit card, or don't pay a bill, or take out a loan or borrow from a friend, then you're just kidding yourself that you have more money than you really do. If you are constantly depending on debt to get what you want, you're just digging a deeper financial hole which gets harder and harder to get out of.

The worst thing about having any form of debt is that it destroys your options. Each time you increase your debt you effectively eliminate more options - but the good news is, the reverse is true too. Each time you reduce your debt or pay another one off, you slowly, bit by bit, get back more options until the day you are debt-free and your options are at an all-time high. **Now that's not just financial freedom; that will give you a sense of true freedom**. There is nothing more empowering than making decisions based on your desires rather than on your bank balance; believe me, I speak from personal experience.

Credit cards are one of the biggest and most insidious forms of debt all around the world. The average person has a real sense of accomplishment and achievement when their credit card application is approved. It's almost as if the bank recognises you have what it takes to pay that money back, whereas in reality, the bank sees you only as a way of increasing its profit margin. Their one and only aim in giving you a credit card, is for you to continue to charge a decent amount of debt and consistently pay only the minimum monthly payments and, hopefully, never be able to pay the balance in full – ever.

I remember the day I got my first credit card. I had just landed my first full time job and applied for a credit card because I wanted to travel to Bali and had to pay for the flights before I'd saved up all the money. I thought putting something on my new credit card would be a one-time thing, I'd pay the money back and that would be that. Little did I know that the debt would continue to accumulate, and for the next 25 years of my life I NEVER paid off my card in full.

And the worst part about it is, if you pay your card off on time you're known among industry insiders as a 'deadbeat' because you aren't paying your share of interest – the company isn't actually making anything out of you. **This is the one time in your life you DO want to be called a deadbeat, and you can be proud of it!**

There is nothing more empowering than making decisions based on your desires rather than on your bank balance.

So the first thing you must do is STOP using your credit card. Make the decision not to go further into debt. Leave it at home, cut it up if you have to, or just make the decision that you won't use it. (I even heard of one lady putting her card in a cup of water and freezing it so she couldn't use it!)

Because I used my credit card for business I couldn't just cut it up, but I found that something called the 24-hour rule worked well for me. If I wanted to use my card, I had to wait 24 hours and think about whether I really needed to purchase that item, whether I could get it cheaper somewhere else, or whether I could go without it altogether. This alone will save you a stack of money. **If you do**

want to continue using your card, there are ways you can use your card appropriately:

◇ Use the 24 hour rule.

◇ Don't carry it with you – if it's not with you can't use it.

◇ Never carry a balance over from one month to the next (be a deadbeat).

◇ When you make a purchase simply for convenience (work for instance or an internet purchase), transfer that money straight onto your card (write a cheque or use internet banking).

◇ When you make a payment onto your card, whether it's the monthly payment or transferring the money each time you use it – always pay an additional $10-$20. This will add up very quickly and you will have your card paid off in no time.

One of the greatest gifts you can give yourself is the freedom from the heavy responsibility of debt. It is such a burden to continually have debt hanging over your head year after year, especially if it just keeps growing bigger and bigger. Understand though, there are actually two types of debt: good debt and bad debt. Money borrowed to purchase investment properties or a business, or anything which is creating on-going income is good debt and not what I consider a heavy responsibility. What we are talking about here is bad debt; debt that doesn't bring you any income or increase your financial situation in any way (purchasing holidays, meals, clothing, food etc on credit card or through a loan).

Take the time to list all the outstanding debts you now intend to pay off. Don't focus on the fact that you owe this money; instead, focus on how wonderful you will feel as you pay off these debts. Feel how amazing you will feel when you are bad-debt free, when you are no longer a slave to your credit card. <u>Make sure you experience the satisfaction of crossing each debt off your list as you attract the money into your life to pay it in full</u>. Believe me, this is one of the most empowering and liberating feelings you will ever experience! Start imagining it in your mind now, and **celebrate when you experience it in your life!**

 Wildly Wealthy Action Tips

Use your credit card responsibly or not at all.

List your debts and see and feel each one as already paid off.

Cross your debts off as you pay them and feel proud of yourself.

See Your Desire, Create Your Desire

'If your faith is in all-sufficiency of supply, then so is your life…
If your faith is on the dial-set of insufficiency,
then there will never be enough to meet your needs.
Your world simply reflects your faith.'
JOHN RANDOLPH PRICE

I used to drive a car that I hadn't looked after and had turned into a bomb. It was really rusty and had a terrible leaking problem – the water would come in through the roof somewhere and sit in puddles on the floor and get that really musty, mouldy smell about it. I live on the Sunshine Coast in tropical Queensland in Australia and when it rains, it really rains! One day after a particularly heavy rainfall, the kids were getting into the car to go to school and my son said to me, "Mum, there's a plant growing in the back of the car". Sure enough, a seed must have been brought in on one of the kids' shoes and with all that wonderful water, a small tree had sprouted overnight. It was about 15cm high already!

It was then that I realised a new car was needed – but I had NO money. I decided to go looking anyway – no harm in dreaming. I liked the idea of a 4WD and a friend had a Rav 4, so I went looking in the local car yards for one like hers. My kids got all excited and came along one day, but as we were driving home we passed the local Landrover yard and stopped for a quick look. My daughter (who I always say was a princess in a past life – she only wants the best of everything!) **decided we should look no further – we had to get the new Landrover Freelander**. Who was I to argue – it looked great. One tiny problem – the car was

$35,000 <u>and I had NO money, was $100,000 in debt and at this point, only bringing in around $18,000 a year!</u>

Nevertheless, I phoned the car dealer the following week and said I was interested in a new car. I had already decided if I got myself a new car, it would be silver. They didn't have one at the yard in the exact shade I wanted, but told me where I could take a look at one. They let me take the little Freelander on a test-drive (I fell in love with it at once – it didn't shake, rattle, clunk, leak or smell like mould like my other car) and

> *The power of pictures should never be underestimated.*

I drove for about twenty minutes to see the car I wanted in my colour. It was perfect, and I had my photo taken lounging all over the car as if it was my own (luckily the owner was not at home or they may have called the police!)

I kept the photo of me and 'my' Freelander on my computer where I could see it all day long. Every time I looked at that picture I knew I would have that car one day; I knew it would be mine. I got excited about that car; **I could remember how it felt, how it smelt and how it looked when I was driving it. I could feel it in my bones** – even though I had NO money.

Less than six months later, I was down at the Landrover yard, picking up my new silver Freelander, when the lady handing me my new keys said, "I bet you're excited" (which I'm sure they say to everyone who comes to pick up their new car). I turned to her and said, "Excited? You have no idea how excited I am. Six months ago I was on the Sole Parent Benefit with over $100,000 in debt and here I am picking up my new Freelander, I've just moved into a beautiful house on the water and I'm about to go to an amazing personal development seminar with a new business I've started that's making me a lot of money. Yes, you could say I'm excited". Believe me, I was thrilled to bits. I had a smile from ear to ear as I drove my new Freelander out of that car yard.

The power of pictures should never be underestimated. I have since used pictures (either those I have taken myself, or others I've cut from magazines) to attract all sorts of wonderful things into my life. If you are visual, like I am, you can use pictures in many wonderful ways. <u>One of the most creative and fun ways is to create a Vision Board.</u> Get yourself a piece of cardboard. Grab some scissors and magazines and begin cutting. Flick through those magazines and when you see a picture, or words that 'make your heart sing', cut them out. You can have pictures for every area of your life – your finances, your weight, your relationship, your looks, your health, your business, your family, your spirituality etc. Take all these pictures and arrange them on your piece of cardboard. **These should all be things you want to attract into your life**.

I remember the first time I put together a vision board. I was at a weekend workshop and we were all told to grab a piece of cardboard. I had big dreams, and took all the left over pieces, eight in total, and joined them together. I put pictures of houses and cars (no not just one of each – many), jewellery, clothes, yachts (what was I thinking, I get seasick!) and all the things I imagined Millionaires to have. It was fun putting it together, but my heart and soul did not feel excited or energised by these pictures – they did not make my heart sing. Plus it was far too big for my wall and so heavy it kept falling down!

When I went back and made another Vision Board about a year later, I included all the things that I really wanted in my life: dolphins jumping out of the sea, sunsets and waterfalls, the moon rising out of the ocean, flowers, people lazing in hammocks, Hawaiian Islands, a briefcase and a map of the world – all things I loved and wanted in my life. Now that was something I could get excited about – that's what I wanted in my life. **Needless to say I have attracted all that and more** – international businesses (the briefcase) many trips overseas including Hawaii (I love to travel), and the time to spend relaxing and connecting with nature. Mind you, I mustn't be focusing enough on my picture of Brad Pitt with long flowing locks from *Legends of the Fall* – he hasn't walked into my life <u>yet</u>!

A Vision Board is a powerful tool and you can get some great photos from the usual magazines. There's no need to go out and buy a lot. You will find friends and family usually have a pile hidden somewhere. Although I do recommend you take the time to ask your newsagent for a couple of inspiring magazines –especially those for

'Rich People'. <u>You will get a real kick out of flicking through</u> *The Robb Report, Millionaire,* or *Connoisseurs Gallery*. They're pricey magazines, and well worth every cent. Make sure you buy each of them at least once. You'll get a glimpse into the world of Multi-Millionaires and Billionaires and the things people with bucket loads of excess cash spend their dollars on! They are a lot of fun to read and will expand your prosperity consciousness at the same time!

I had a friend who once had a subscription to *The Robb Report* and gave me dozens of old copies. My gosh, that was such an eye opener for me and a ton of fun. **The clothes, the jewels, the mansions, the jets, the little doodads that you can spend your money on when you are rich beyond your wildest dreams are simply amazing.** Start putting together your pictures now, so they can become a reality in your life.

 Wildly Wealthy Action Tips

Take a photo of something you want in your life – look at it often.

Create a Vision Board.

Words for Your Abundance

'Ask and it shall be given you: seek and ye shall find:
knock and it shall be opened unto you.
For everyone that asketh receiveth: and he that seeketh findeth
and to him that knocketh it shall be opened'
MATTHEW 7:7

Another great visual tip is to print out some of your affirmations and **place them around your house/work space where you can see them**. I have a lot of fun creating affirmations with different fonts on the computer – I find really bright coloured paper and make the writing as big as will fit on one sheet.

I often cut those printed affirmations out in different shapes if there is enough space around the words (maybe hearts or circles) and then place them where I know I will see them often. You see, your mind is a wondrous tool. **You don't have to go up to each affirmation every single day and read it word by word for it to be driven deeper into your subconscious.** Your eyes don't only see what you are looking at directly. Stick these affirmations on your kitchen cupboards, bathroom mirror, bedroom walls, the dashboard of your car and near your computer – everywhere you spend time – and <u>your subconscious mind will constantly be absorbing them, even when you're busy doing other things</u>.

I remember having an affirmation on my wall once that said something along the lines of, "I see a person drawn into my life immediately who will empower me to run my business with tremendous finesse. They are honest, ethical and we create synergy and success that attracts millions". After writing it and putting it up on my bedroom wall, I never really read it again. The thing is, **every time I was in that room, my eyes were taking it all in.** The result of simply writing this affirmation and having it there for my subconscious mind to continually absorb was amazing – as you'll see a little later!

And remember, you can write affirmations about any area of your life. Maybe you'd like to be a certain weight, or have a relationship with someone special or look a little differently. Maybe you want more balance in your life or better health. **All this and more can be achieved through writing it down concisely** _____ **and precisely and feeding that information on a consistent basis to your subconscious.**

> *I love the freedom of being able to do what I want when I want, work only when I feel like it, doing only what really inspires me!*

When I decided that I had to show the Universe I was committed to making changes in my financial situation, and I would do ANYTHING (well, almost anything) to get out of my horrid money mess and make things better, I knew it was time to get a job.

Now this is not something I did lightly. I had not had a job for about 20 years – that's not because I'm some sort of lazy bum, it's because I had always been a bit of an entrepreneur, always liked to do my own thing, always trying something new. **I love the freedom of being able to do what I want when I want, work only when I feel like it, doing only what really inspires me.** So to go out and get a job seemed like a huge step down for me. The very fact that I had to go to work in the morning stay there all day until I was told I could leave was like being in jail – it was suffocating. But I found a casual position fairly quickly, running a men's clothing outlet. It was on the Esplanade, opposite the beach, so the first day at work seemed like a breeze. It was really quiet with only a few customers all day, so I had plenty of time on my hands.

It almost seemed too good to be true because it was so quiet that I had time to read my inspiring books and write my goals, AND I still got paid. "Maybe a job isn't such a bad thing after all", I thought.

But by the second day the thrill had worn off; I felt like I was in a straight jacket, but as much as I hated it, I really desperately needed the money, so I stayed. During this time I decided to once again write out **my ideal,** but this time instead of my ideal day – I wrote about <u>my ideal business</u>:

◊ One that allowed me to work from home, or elsewhere if I chose

◊ One that had a great product with a huge profit margin

◊ One that allowed me to choose my own hours and work part time

◊ One that allowed me to travel overseas if I wanted

◊ One that made me over $1000 a week (my confidence was a little shaky so my goals were a little low)

◊ One that I really enjoyed.

Funnily enough, once I'd written out that list the first thing that popped into my mind was Real Estate. So I thought to myself, "Although I don't really like the idea of being a real estate agent, maybe I can make a lot of money out of it, get out of debt and then go on to other things", so I did some research and sent away for a Real Estate Sales course that I could do by correspondence in my own time around my new job.

It was about this time that I received a phone call from my accountant who wanted to talk with me about 'doing something together'. Coincidently, (<u>let me tell you here and now there are no coincidences; everything is meant to be!</u>) it was a business marketing Real Estate Education, teaching people how to make money investing in Real Estate. The company was aligned with one of the world's greatest investors and sounded very interesting. Although my logical mind was saying, "Stay away, you said you'd never get into sales again – don't do it!"– My heart was saying, "Yes, this feels good, this feels right, this will lead you places". So I began that business with my new business partner and **within a few weeks had to let my employer know that I simply couldn't work any longer** (I was making SO MUCH

MONEY at my new business and it was school holidays and I really wanted to be home to be with my kids!).

So my career as an employee lasted just over a month – but I guess that was just long enough for the Universe to see how serious I really was and start the flow of riches to me!

That new business marketing a Real Estate Educational Package was a lot of fun and I made a lot of money and learnt a lot about real estate investing, but ultimately it was a stepping stone for something even bigger and better than anything even I could have ever imagined! Through having that affirmation on my bedroom wall (the one I hardly read) I was able to attract someone into my life, and together we created a synergy that has allowed us to build a business that empowers women around the world to create the life of their dreams. **Wildly Wealthy Women** is a life changing mentoring program that allows women to energise their body, empower their mind and enlighten their spirit, as well as expand their wealth.

> *There are no coincidences; everything is meant to be.*

And the best part is – my new business partner is not only a highly successful property investor, she's an Asset Protection and Taxation expert and an Accountant; she knows numbers inside out, so my mathematically challenged brain doesn't even have to think about that side of things! Our skills and talents complement each other perfectly. She teaches women the practical side to creating wealth and I teach the metaphysical, the 'woo woo', the millionaire mindset. We like to think of ourselves as the Yin and Yang of Wealth Creation. We have a load of fun doing what we do best and have hundreds of women attending our **Wildly Wealthy Women's Wicked Weekends**, where they learn lots of practical wealth creation ideas, along with many steps for them to create their Millionaire Mindset. During our time together, **we enjoy visualization, meditation, yoga and other expansive and enjoyable activities** for a really exciting, fun, empowering, life-changing experience. You can visit www.WildlyWealthyWomen.com to find out more if you want to join in the fun!

Our Millionaire Mentoring Program with Wildly Wealthy Women is everything I would love to have seen in the dozens of events I've attended. And the stories from the women who are now transforming their lives – not just financially, but personally as well – is the most amazing part of all. **I am doing what I love to do – sharing my story, my secrets and my strategies with thousands of women around the world to give them courage and hope and help them to dream bigger, desire grander, imagine more and go out there and achieve it.** <u>I have found my life's purpose and it is more than I could ever have imagined.</u>

Even if you have no idea what you can do (I have some tips for you later in the book), or if you do know what it is and have no idea how to make it happen, don't get caught up in the details. Remember, if the Universe can re-arrange the entire cosmos, it can shuffle a few things around in your world to make your dreams come true. **Just be clear on what it is you want, and let the Universe take care of the details.** My dream came true all from some simple words on my bedroom wall – and it can happen for you too!

> *If the Universe can re-arrange the entire cosmos, it can shuffle a few things around in your world to make your dreams come true!*

Wildly Wealthy Action Tip

Place your Affirmations where you will see them constantly so they become imprinted on your subconscious.

Let the Universe Do its Job!

'The Universe is all about increase,
about growth about abundance.
For you to be and do and have all you can be,
do and have, you must be Rich.'
WALLACE D. WATTLES

There are two different ways (with lots of variations) to attract all you desire into your life. You can do it:

1. through the head – with repetition

2. through the heart – with emotion and feeling

As previously stated, manifesting through the head is when you think about something over and over; when you repeat something over and over, when you continually say it, see it, focus on it. **It can sometimes seem to be hard work, but it definitely works.**

I have manifested some wonderful things into my life through constant repetition of affirmations and other techniques you are learning in this book, so I know you will get results that way. The downside is it can take a little longer (sometimes a lot longer). And quite often what happens is, while you are waiting around for your desire to appear – you start to question if this actually works. You may begin to doubt that you will get the results you are seeking, you stop doing the head work and **take your focus off what you want**. You begin instead, to **look at how things currently are**, which is **exactly what you must not do** – because that's **when you 'cancel the order' at your warehouse**. So while repetition does work, there is an easier way!

Manifesting through the heart is more magical, easier, faster and far more powerful. Thinking (the head work) about your greatest desire, and energizing it with emotions (through the heart) is what gives your desire life. They both attract your desires to you, but when you do them both at once, the power is magnified. There is a great exercise later in the book that will help you to tap into that amazing power. Once you are clear on what you want, and I can't say this enough, **get your logical mind out of the way**. Don't try and figure out how it will happen. Don't try to step all the steps through to achieving your dream. Let all that go, let the Universe figure out how it will make it happen. Let the Universe devise the most exciting, fun and eventful way to make your dreams come true.

I remember having a trip to Hawaii organised. I had finally saved up enough money for the airfare to complete the last event of a three-part course with Anthony Robbins. The day before I was due to leave I had a phone call from someone who told me about a beautiful bay about an hour away from where I was staying on Kona, "Where, if you are lucky" she said, "you can swim with the dolphins". I LOVE dolphins; they are beautiful, strong, sensitive, empowered creatures. There is something magical about them that moves me whenever I see one. She told me how I would have to organise transport as well as hire out kayaks and underwater gear to get the most out of the experience. There was no time to find out all the details but I REALLY wanted to swim with the dolphins.

> *Manifesting through the heart is more magical, easier, faster and far more powerful.*

When I arrived at Kona, I made some enquiries but, my gosh, the trip to that special bay was definitely in the too hard basket. I decided to go on a local trip where they said we might see dolphins. I had a great day out in the ocean diving in the warm tropical waters amongst the lava spills and brightly coloured fish, but there were no dolphins to be seen. I didn't care (much). As I gently swayed underwater to the ocean rhythm, I imagined I could see dolphins swimming around me and it filled me with such powerful emotions of love, it was almost as good as actually having them there with me.

I still had in the back of my mind that I would love to swim with the dolphins in that special bay, but with the event starting around nine o'clock each morning and ending around midnight or later, there was NO chance to organise anything; maybe I'd be able to organise it on the last day, which was a free day.

The week passed, and on the last day of the event I was walking up the huge stairs of the Hilton Waikoloa Village and glanced up – a man walking down the stairs caught my eye and said hello. I smiled and said hello back, and then he stopped on the stairs next to me. I didn't want to be rude, so I stopped too. He asked me why there were so many people around (about 1200) and I told him it was an Anthony Robbins event, it was the last day and we were graduating tonight. He thought that was great, because he'd been through the same training and loved it. He asked me what else I'd been doing, and I told him about my ocean swim, and mentioned how no dolphins had shown up.

Let the Universe devise the most exciting, fun and eventful way to make your dreams come true.

He then told me how he lived down by a bay (the one that had the dolphins) and that, if I wanted, he'd love to take me there and maybe I could see the dolphins after all. Keep in mind, I am in a strange country, I don't know this man from Adam, and he's inviting me to travel over 100km away with him for the day. My logical mind went into overdrive – "No way, this man could be a serial killer, don't even think about it" – but my creative mind said: "The Universe has set this up; don't let a great opportunity go by – with more than two thousand people in this hotel, you just 'happened' to cross paths". But my logical mind won out and I told him I didn't think so because I didn't want him to drive all the way back here to get me (the only excuse I could come up with!). He then said "You should, it would be perfect, I'm a yoga teacher here at the Hilton, and I have a class tomorrow morning. I could pick you up after the class and we could spend the day there and I could bring you back afterwards". By this time my hormones were winning over my logical mind as I was thinking, "Yoga teacher, good looking, cute smile – I'm there!" So we organised that he would meet me at the front of the hotel the next morning.

At the appointed time, he pulled up outside the hotel in a fancy little red sports car. He jumped out, opened my door and handed me the most divine lei I had ever seen, made from wild orchids. He told me it was a congratulations gift for graduating from my seminar, as he knew it was a big accomplishment. We drove away into the warm summer day, and when we reached the next town, he took me to a supermarket and told me to buy whatever I wanted for our picnic lunch. We piled back into the car with shopping bags full, and after more driving and talking he then pulled into a little sports store on the side of the road. When we got out, I realised we were there to hire kayaks and snorkels, goggles and flippers to use during our day. "Oh my gosh", I'm thinking to myself, "is this real? It's all falling into place so easily!"

And that's the exact thing. <u>When you are connected, energized and your vibration is pure and high, you will be in the flow; things will happen with little effort; everything just seems to fall into place</u>. That's what flow is all about; that's what being a co-creator is all about.

The Yoga teacher and I had the most wonderful day in this beautiful bay. No dolphins showed up, but it didn't matter because there was no-one else but us swimming amongst the thousands of tropical fish. We sat with our feet dangling in the water munching on yummy chocolate chip cookies, drinking orange juice and eating pineapple. We spent hours talking, laughing and really enjoying ourselves.

Now do you think for a moment that I could have organised all those events and circumstances to happen and put it all perfectly into place? Not in a million years. The Universe has tricks up its sleeve you don't even know about. **You just have to be clear on what it is you want, imagine it as already real then let it go and let the Universe do its thing**. Stop trying to manage the Universe and just manage yourself and your mind. The Universe knows what it's doing and really doesn't need you to map out every step of its grand plan for you. <u>It just needs you to know what it is you want, and it will work out the best way to get it to you!</u>

And to top it off, the hotel where I was staying had a dolphin training program and they had a competition where you could win a special session swimming with the dolphins in their huge free form dolphin pool. And when I returned to the hotel, I had won just that – so I got to swim with not only grown dolphins, but with two baby dolphins that were only three days old. It was a magical experience and I thanked the Universe for giving me all I desired – and more!

You too can attract all you desire and much, much more when you create the emotions you would feel as if it is already 'a done deal'. It works every time, in ways you can't even begin to imagine! Understand that the Universe loves you, more than you could possibly imagine; <u>it wants you to be happy, it wants to give you your greatest desires, it wants to make your dreams come true</u>. Place your order and let the Universe do its thing!

 Wildly Wealthy Action Tip

Resign as Manager of the Universe; know what you want and let the Universe take over.

Raise Your Vibration

'Shoot for the moon.
Even if you miss, you will land among the stars.'
LES BROWN

Feelings are everything; they are the key when it comes to creating. Feelings will attract your desires to you and feelings will repel them. Some feelings will speed your desires into your life and others will block your desires altogether. Abundance is your natural state. The way that you feel is your indicator of whether you are letting in that flow – that abundance that is natural to you and always there for you – or whether you are pushing it away.

If you are feeling expansive and light then you will be able to attract the Abundance you desire; if you feel contracted and heavy, then it will be an uphill battle. As I have said many times over, **what you focus on is what you create**. Rather than continually monitoring your thoughts and words, <u>it is actually far easier if you focus on the feelings and actions that expand your energy and raise your vibration</u>. Start by doing things that make you feel good. When you feel good, you naturally begin thinking empowering thoughts and saying things that uplift you; you automatically become magnetic to your dreams. **Life becomes easy; you get in the flow**.

There are many benefits to being in a high vibrational state:

◊ You feel energised and radiant

◊ You feel supported, safe and secure

◊ You become empowered

◊ You experience increased clarity and awareness

◊ You feel alive and free

◊ You effortlessly achieve more balance in life

◊ You take on a youthful glow and a childlike exuberance

◊ You are confident and enthusiastic

◊ You experience improved health

◊ You experience synchronicity consistently

◊ You get in the flow and life becomes easy

◊ You consistently think and feel empowering emotions

There are many ways to raise your energy, or vibration, but the most important is to honour yourself. I once read, "The Universe will only look after you to the extent you look after yourself." Meaning, if you think so lowly of yourself that you eat rubbish, take toxins into your body, are overweight, unorganised, stressed

> *If you are feeling expansive and light then you will be able to attract the Abundance you desire!*

and living in chaos, then **you are making a strong statement to the Universe**. And that statement is you don't think you're worth much – and that's exactly what you will attract back into your life – not much!

So it makes sense to take excellent care of yourself. Your body is your temple – treat it as one. If you don't look after your body, where are you going to live? All those things you've heard about eating your vegetables, getting enough sleep and drinking more water are more than just Mum's ranting and raving about feeling good – they are magical things that will increase your vibration and make you more attractive to prosperity, abundance and wealth! As you raise your vibration you get in the flow and things begin to happen easily and effortlessly. You experience synchronicity or meaningful coincidences.

Do these things to honour yourself every day and your energy or vibration will automatically rise:

◇ Spend that quiet time each day in quiet contemplation or prayer, whatever feels right for you.

◇ Learn to Meditate, it is a powerful skill that will transform your life

◇ Exercise and look after your physical self – the better you feel physically, the higher vibration you will naturally be.

◇ Organize and beautify your surroundings – get rid of clutter and things you don't use. Turn off the TV and listen to uplifting music.

◇ Nourish your body with life-giving foods – as within, so without. The more alive and energized you are on the inside, the more you will be on the outside. Your world without – in every way – reflects the world within.

◇ Reduce toxins from your life – alcohol, cigarettes, sugar, and stress.

◇ Drink more water – water helps remove toxins from your body; just by drinking more water you find you lose weight, are more alert and feel more energized.

◇ Rest when you feel tired and get a peaceful nights sleep.

◇ Feed your mind with uplifting, inspiring and growth-oriented information – throw away the magazines and newspapers; read books that make you magnetic to prosperity and happiness and **it will be yours**.

Show the Universe that you value you. Once you value you more – you will find more will flow to you.

Here are some more things to focus on that will expand your energy and raise your vibration:

◇ Feeling connected to and supported by the Universe

◇ Being enthusiastic

◇ Having massages

◇ Taking Action

◊ Loving yourself and loving others

◊ Feeling grateful

◊ Laughing

◊ Feeling Joy

◊ Praising others and accepting praise

◊ Any form of energy work – Reiki, Reflexology etc.

◊ Saying empowering affirmations

◊ Creating a void through clearing clutter – in your house, car, cupboards, garage etc.

◊ Thinking uplifting and inspiring thoughts

◊ Accepting love

◊ Feeling deserving

◊ Spending time in nature

◊ Having fun

◊ Doing what you love

◊ Singing and dancing

◊ Playing silly games with your children or friends

◊ Listening to empowering CDs

◊ Cuddling your kids

◊ Spending time with a positive friends

◊ Connecting to a like-minded Mastermind

◊ Feeling the joy in being alive, being a creator, being the designer of your future and knowing that anything is possible!

When you raise your vibration and then apply the techniques in this book, your results will appear so much faster than if you try and create from a low vibrational state. On a metaphysical level it's difficult to take action when you are feeling heavy and your vibration is slow.

Think of that statement **from a purely physical perspective**: If you were suddenly selected to run (or walk) a 500km marathon and would receive $1,000,000 just for finishing, I'm sure you'd attempt to do it. But more than likely it would be a long and arduous journey. You may even feel like giving up along the way. You would wonder if you were ever going to make it. You would eventually get there, but it might take you 10 times longer than someone who was ready for such a challenge.

Let's say on the other hand, you were not only eating well, exercising daily, getting plenty of sleep and generally looking after your 'temple', you were also training to run a marathon some time in the future. If you had the same $1,000,000 challenge, you would jump at the chance with wild enthusiasm. And yes, it may still be very challenging – but I bet you would <u>get there a whole lot quicker</u>.

> *Your world without*
>
> *– in every way –*
>
> *reflects the world within!*

That's exactly how it works on the metaphysical plane. If you are 'training' for wealth by **raising your vibration AND implementing the strategies in this book, you will find it comes a whole lot quicker!** There is a connection – the Body, Mind, Spirit connection. One affects the other; it's all about balance. Nourish yourself physically, empower your mind and uplift your spirit. <u>When you nurture all three, you will naturally energise your attracting powers!</u>

So open your arms to a life of Prosperity by loving yourself and your body – **look after yourself, do what makes you happy and you will see the abundance flood into your life!**

 Wildly Wealthy Action Tips

Honour yourself – body, mind and spirit.

Do whatever you can to raise your vibration.

Where is YOUR Money Going?

'If your outgo exceeds your income,
then your upkeep will be your downfall.'

BILL EARLE

When I said the Universe loves order, I meant it! If you are so 'messy' with your money that you don't know what is coming in and what is going out then you will have a challenge becoming wealthy. You will find it difficult to keep what little money you already have, but even worse, **your energy will probably be pushing money away** before it even comes into your reality.

If you are committed to achieving abundance, then this strategy will allow you to break free of financial confusion and distress. If you are financially 'messy', you will understand me totally when I say it's almost impossible to change your thinking when you're pressured with unpaid bills and debts; when

> *Getting control of how you handle money gives you a new perspective and a new energy to attract more of it.*

you're undisciplined in the way you work with money. **Getting control of how you handle money gives you a new perspective and a new energy to attract more of it!**

I used to be unconscious when it came to spending. If you had asked me a couple of years ago how much petrol (gas) cost, or how much a carton of milk or a loaf of bread was – I would have had to say, "I have no idea"; because I didn't. I honestly didn't take any notice of how much was flowing in and out of my life. I just knew I seemed to have enough (or seemed to on the surface) whereas in fact, I was racking up a lot of unpaid bills, credit card debt and my overdraft was getting bigger and bigger. I guess it was safer for me to ignore it all.

For instance, I would go to the corner store, buy some bread, maybe grab a magazine and a chocolate bar at the same time, hand over my money, get my change, put it in my wallet and walk out. If you then immediately asked me how much I had just spent – I wouldn't have had a clue. **I just knew that I had less money in my wallet walking out of that shop, than I had walking in**.

Too often when it comes to money, it is almost scarier facing exactly where you are than just ignoring it and hoping for the best. That's definitely where I was. What I have since discovered is this – **if you can combine knowing exactly where you are financially on a consistent basis AND hope for the best, your money-attracting powers will be greatly multiplied; you will find you attract more money and at a faster rate if you can get clear on where you are now with what you DO have**.

You really need to get clear on what your money is doing, and the first step to that is <u>knowing where your money is going.</u>

This was a very challenging step for me, but once it was done it was very freeing to have a clear picture of where my money was going, because it meant I could consciously make changes for the better. I could be in control of my money and my life, instead of my money controlling me. And believe me, no matter how much or how little money you have, this is a very liberating feeling! **This will allow you to break free of the financial confusion and distress you may be experiencing.**

As I said, the first part of knowing what your money is doing is knowing where your money is going; <u>knowing exactly what you are spending your money on.</u> Knowing what your money is doing and where it is going initially can seem rather messy and out of control. It almost seems to make things worse before it makes things better. Not always mind you, but it definitely did in my case.

Let me give you an example. Let's say you decide to get rid of all the clutter in your garage. It's been stored there, away from sight for years – but there is a part of you that knows it's there, and every time you are in that garage you expend energy (on an unconscious level) around that mess. So you finally decide to do something about it. You put aside a whole weekend and get those stored boxes down from the shelves, and dig out that clutter of old garden tools and sports equipment and go through them. You make a pile of things you want to keep, you make a pile of things you are going to donate to charity, you make another pile of things you will throw out and yet another pile of things you're not too sure of just yet.

As the day progresses and you find more and more things stored away in cupboards and behind boxes and underneath benches, you have items and rubbish spread from one end of the garage to the next and even strewn out across the driveway and the lawn. The garage and front yard of your home looks like a bomb hit it. You begin to wish you had never started. You wish you had just left it as it was – it may have been taking up a little extra space, but at least you weren't in the middle of this chaos! You feel overwhelmed and just want to close the garage door and walk away from it all. But bit-by-bit you keep going and slowly those piles begin to take shape. The charity truck turns up and takes your donations away, you throw all the rubbish in the bin (and in your friendly neighbours' bins too, you had so much) and you realise that you're starting to get on top of it, you're starting to feel there is some order taking shape – there is light at the end of the tunnel.

By the end of the weekend you are beaming with pride. Your garage has twice the amount of space, you feel lighter on an energetic level because you have cleared so much clutter, and you feel proud that you have sorted out that mess, which will now allow you to keep on top of things for another year or so.

This is how it can be when you decide to take control over your finances. **When you take that first long, hard look at where you are financially so you can take steps to clean things up, it can be very scary; it can get very messy and sometimes you wish you had just let things be and kept floating along with your head in the sand.** That's what it was like for me when I actually had to stop and take stock of how much was coming in and how much was going out and where it was all actually going. I realised that if I continued down the same track for another minute longer, I would be just getting further and further in debt.

Once you make that decision to be in control of your finances it is extremely empowering to put practical steps into place so you become the master of your money, rather than remain a slave to what little money you have!

The first part of knowing what your money is doing is to begin writing down everything you spend, <u>down to the last cent.</u> When I first heard this technique, part of me wanted to do it, I had made the decision to be responsible, to take control of my finances, to totally transform my life into one of abundance and riches, so I thought to myself, "I will do this starting tomorrow. I will write down everything I spend, because once I know where it's going I'll be able to make changes and improvements".

Now that's what I thought on a conscious level, but part of me must have been resisting so hard, because even though I'd made that decision, it was more than two months before I managed to write down everything I spent for a whole day! Let's hope it doesn't take you that long, because the **sooner you know where your money is going, the sooner you can make better decisions about where it will go.**

<u>The great thing about this strategy is your logical brain gets so excited that you are actually doing something practical towards creating wealth.</u> For once your analytical side has something to focus on and keep it occupied, and because it doesn't try and interfere with your creative mind as you are doing your manifesting techniques – **you can actually get better, faster results!** Plus, as an added bonus, and once again on a subconscious level, you are affirming to yourself that you DO know how to handle money, that you CAN be responsible with money and you ARE ready to accept larger and larger amounts of cash into your life. **This very practical step actually allows you to free up the energy you hold around money, so you attract more of it into your life, easily and effortlessly.**

For you to know where you can make changes and improvements in your financial situation, you have to have to know where to start. It's like saying you want to travel to Wealth City, but you have no idea where you are right now. It's going to be a much faster ride if you can figure out exactly where you are now!

I always liken each cent you spend to each bite you eat. Let's say you really were dedicated to losing weight and decided to write down everything you consumed and every bit of exercise you did, so you could see exactly how many calories were going in and exactly how many were being expended. If, you then thought, "well, I won't worry about writing down that bit of Johnny's donut, it isn't enough to make any difference, and that half a sandwich I polished off after the kids finished lunch wasn't much, and that leftover bit of orange juice could hardly make any difference, I won't bother recording that", while each little bit individually doesn't make any difference, when it's all added up, it can be the difference between losing the weight you want and staying overweight forever. It's the same with transforming your financial picture – **every little bit can make a huge difference to the final outcome.** So the plan is to write it ALL down!

When I say write it down – I mean you must write down everything you spend, and I do mean everything. Even that 50c you spent on a lollipop for your son or the 20c you put in a parking meter. You must write **it all** down. You won't need to do it forever; this is just your starting point to having a good understanding of where your money is going now. With this essential information you can work out where to make changes and get where you want to be financially, much faster.

There are a few different ways to keep track of your money; you may prefer the Envelope Method. This is where you carry an envelope with you at all times and put in your receipt every time you spend money. You may also need paper and a pen to jot down those items that you don't receive a receipt for (kids' bus money or a parking meter).

Or maybe you'd prefer the Notebook Method. Keep a pen and notebook in your wallet or purse, and write down every purchase.

My preferred method is the Analysis Book. I bought an 18-column accounts book from an office supplies store, and tracked my money in that. This is easy for me because I work from home, so if I give my children money, I am usually at home when I do so. If I spend any money at a shop, I then usually go home fairly soon afterwards, so it's really easy to write it down (then why did it take me two months to do this for a whole day?) I keep all my receipts whenever I spend money, and I write the details down every time I come home, so at the end of every day I have that whole day already accounted for. Then at the end of the month, I total each column up so I can see where the money is going.

I once had a client who was so busy with young children, she said there was no way she could find two spare hands to write down what she spent while she was out shopping, so she had a **mini recorder and would track each purchase that way**. You can also use a computer program to track your money if you're that way inclined, lots of my clients use Quicken or something similar – although that's in the too hard basket for me!

The great thing about tracking your money is you can then clearly see where your money is going and decide to make better choices. For instance, across the top of my 18 columns, I had headings such as Food, Clothing, Take-away, Entertainment, Children, Petrol, Rent, Chocolate. "Why chocolate?" you might ask. Well, everyone has a vice, and it can be very eye-opening to see just how much you are spending on something that is not particularly good for you. My vice is chocolate. I know I eat too much of it, but I don't drink alcohol, don't smoke and have never been a tea or coffee drinker, so I thought being aware of how much I was spending on chocolate might be a good thing. It turned out to

> *Everyone has a vice, and it can be very eye-opening to see just how much you are spending on something that is not particularly good for you.*

be an EXCELLENT thing, because just by knowing that I had to write down every chocolate bar I was spending my money on (and then eating) I thought twice about actually buying chocolate. So over the course of the next couple of months, I actually saved myself almost $200 (yes I was eating a large block most days) and the added bonus is that I lost around 4kg! (10lbs)

So what is YOUR vice? Think about it for a moment, and then give it its own column. It may be chocolate like mine; it may be alcohol or cigarettes or perhaps it's buying magazines. Whatever it is, give it (or them if you have more than one) its own place so you can see very clearly what is being spent. **It may make you think twice about outlaying so much on that item** once you have tracked exactly how much you are spending each month.

The idea behind tracking your money is to add each column up at the end of the month to give you your totals – that will give you a clear picture of where your money is currently going. While this won't be the full picture as you will have other commitments that only occur on a quarterly or yearly basis (insurance, repairs, school fees, holidays, new tyres, phone, electricity, birthday and Christmas presents etc.) it will give you a starting point. If you then continue to track your money over the next year, you will have a very clear indication of what is happening with your money and **will be excited by being in the position to make better choices about what you spend your money on**.

You will find this particularly empowering once you continue your Financial Education and learn how to make the money you have, multiply; **you will no longer look at $100 or even $10 as that single amount of money**. You will see it as part of your financial freedom; you will see it as part of the $1000, or the $10,000 or the $100,000 that will ultimately give you the financial freedom you have been seeking. You will begin to realise that every dollar that comes your way is a precious gift from God, and you will nurture each dollar and help it grow and multiply so you can become rich beyond your wildest dreams!

Wildly Wealthy Action Tips

Track your money.

Go to www.WildlyWealthy.com to download your 'Tracking Money' sheet.

Magical Manifesting Muscle

'If one advances confidently in the direction of his dreams,
and endeavours to live the life which he has imagined,
he will meet with a success unexpected in common hours.'
H.D. Thoreau

Remember, you can manifest what you want through the head with repetition and through the heart with feeling and emotion. Both work; both are great; although your results will be quicker and stay longer if you do both.

To magnify your attracting powers, you first need to practise what manifesting through the heart feels like. It's best if you practise this daily until you are able to feel these emotions easily and quickly whenever you want to. And make sure you have fun with it!

Go to your bedroom at a time you know you won't be disturbed, close the door and lie on the bed.

Get nice and comfy and close your eyes.

◊ Now begin to feel love in your heart.

◊ You may have to think back to when you madly, deliciously, deliriously, joyously loved someone.

◊ It could be your first love; it could be your current love; it could be someone you would love to love; it could be the love of your children.

◊ Think about when you **truly loved, and was loved back** – not just in love, but truly, totally, **unconditionally loved**.

◊ **The idea is to feel that feeling of love; feel it warm your heart**.

◇ Connect to that love; tap into it; feel it and send it back out again.

◇ Stir up all those emotions and all those feelings.

◇ **Feel your heart open** – feel the love flow into your heart.

◇ Feel the love flow through you.

◇ Feel the love flow through you to another.

◇ Feel how wonderful and peaceful and safe and cared for you feel as your heart opens and expands to accept the love flowing to you and how loving you feel as you flow that love back.

◇ **Feel a warmth grow around your heart and begin to flow through you** and expand out through your body.

◇ Now begin to feel that connection, that love coming from the Universe, the Divine, Spirit, God, All That Is.

◇ Begin to experience that feeling, that stirring in your heart.

◇ **Know you are loved fully, totally, unconditionally**.

◇ You are here because you were loved into being.

◇ Feel that love flow between you and the Universe; feel the flow to you; feel you flowing it back.

◇ Feel your heart open; feel how good that feels.

◇ Tap into that power; flow that power back.

◇ **Keep the flow going**.

◇ Bathe in that feeling of love flowing **from the Universe to you and through you**.

◇ Lie there and enjoy that feeling for as long as you desire.

When you're ready, slowly open your eyes and gently sit up. Know that **you can tap into that amazing attracting energy at any time.**

This is working what I call your **'magical manifesting muscle'. It's like polishing your own magic wand.** Just keep practising feeling that love flow, because <u>love is the most powerful of all emotions and has the strongest attracting qualities</u>. Do this exercise daily. It doesn't have to be for a long time. Just a couple of minutes is fine. Once you can feel those strong, loving feelings and you can get there easily, begin to do it at other times (not only on the bed). Just take a moment during your day to stop, open your heart and feel the love flow through you. When you can easily tap into this loving emotion, **use that same energy to begin to attract what you desire.**

Think about what it is you want to bring into your life. Feel the energy of love, feel the love flowing, then attach that same feeling to already having what it is you want in your life. Feel the love you would experience if you already had your desire in your life right now. **Your love will energize your desire so much that it will begin to take on a life all of its own.** **Your desire will gain incredible life force, which causes it to be created very quickly.**

> *Your love will energize your desire so much that it will begin to take on a life all of its own!*

The intention behind utilising this powerful 'magical manifesting muscle' is to experience the enjoyment and appreciation of your desire right now – not at some time in the future. <u>If you fill your vision, your desire, with feelings of appreciation, love, gratitude and enjoyment, those light-hearted feelings will strengthen it and charge it with tremendous life.</u> The powerful Law of Attraction will have no choice but to bring you your desire, just like it brought me mine. It HAS to work!

 Wildly Wealthy Action Tip

Exercise your Magical Manifesting Muscle by feeling love flowing through you – from you and to you – and then envelope your desires in that same feeling.

Go to <u>www.WildlyWealthy.com</u> and listen to your Magical Manifesting Muscle Audio.

Gateway to Your Wealth

'How small the cosmos, how paltry and puny
in comparison to human consciousness.'

VLADIMIR NABOKOV

If you take the time before doing the exercises outlined in this book, or before reading each chapter, to slow down your body and breathing, relax and 'chill out' **you will multiply the benefit you receive from the information.** At the base of your brain is a little gateway called the Reticular Activating System, and it is the gateway between the conscious and the subconscious mind. That gateway acts as a filtering system and only allows into your subconscious that which you consider important. For instance, if I were to tell you to look around the room you are in at this moment, depending on whether you're in the bedroom, lounge room, office etc, you are going to see a number of items. If someone were to ask me that question when I'm in my bedroom, I would say "I can see a bed, the floor, the walls, windows, doors, ceiling fan, a bedside table and lamp, pillows, sheets, wall paintings" and I could probably prattle off 50 things, if I really looked hard, maybe even 100 or more.

What you need to understand is that your conscious mind is only seeing that which you find important. In other words if I was to look around my bedroom again, and I mean really look, I would add that "My bed is wooden, it's got 4 big turned bed ends, the wood is re-cycled so it has many different shades ranging from light brown through to black through it. Because it's re-cycled, there are holes in the wood and scratches all over it, and the wood itself has a grain running through it" and on and on I could go.

If I were to look out the window at the garden I could say, "I see a palm tree outside, and it's green. It's a very light green where the sun shines through the leaf and makes it glow and it's darker as the fronds join to the stem. The spine of the leaf is almost golden and there are long fronds and shorter new brighter green fronds, and it has little marks where a grasshopper has been chewing and there are spider-webs strung between the lower palm fronds, and the breeze is making the fronds sway to and fro and sometimes they move quickly and other times slowly, and there are shadows dancing all over the ground from the sun shining on the fronds" and again on and on I could go.

So if you were to shut your eyes right now, and when you opened them, your brain had to consciously process all that information of every little tiny solitary thing you could see, every time you opened your eyes – it would go into overload, it would shutdown, it would blow a fuse, it simply couldn't cope. **And that's only ONE sense – if you were to include sound, touch, taste and smell – wow – you can now get an insight as to why we have this special filter in our brain.**

So the RAS helps you filter out what you don't need to process on a conscious level – you're still processing it, but you're unaware of it. It only lets you become consciously aware of the things you believe are important to you. <u>This is very useful to know and quite a powerful thing, because you can feed to your subconscious what we DO consider important</u>, so that your conscious mind is aware of those things in your life and you're able to notice things you would otherwise have missed.

Let me give you an example, which I'm sure you've heard before. Let's say you decide you want a new car – a VW Beetle. Once you make that decision, you will be surprised at how many Beetles you see on the road – suddenly there are VWs driving around all over the place. The thing is, they were there all the time, but before, it wasn't important to you. And now that you consider them important, you see them everywhere.

Another example of how this works: I remember when I was 15, I'd just come back from Europe with my family, and had bought a traditional gypsy embroidered blouse made of cheesecloth, it was really pretty and I loved it. That particular style had just come into fashion and I was incredibly proud of that blouse because it was 'the real thing'. I wore it everywhere and it eventually became so threadbare it just fell apart.

A couple of years ago a few months before Christmas, I noticed girls wearing that style; it was the fashion once again. I was seeing them everywhere (deep subconscious patterns can be there for life!), but apparently my daughter, who was thirteen at the time, hadn't yet noticed them. Then, just before Christmas, my daughter and her friend bought one of these blouses. I picked the girls up from the beach one afternoon and they were talking in the back of the car saying "Nobody was wearing these tops until we bought one, and now everybody is. I'm not saying that we started the fashion, but isn't it strange how once we bought one, now everybody's wearing them". That's a perfect example of the RAS at work. Once they considered it important, something they simply did not see previously, is now popping up all over the place, they see it everywhere.

What this means to you is, **if you program your subconscious mind with what is important, for instance, money making opportunities, more clients, certain type of (better) client, new job, increased income** – those things that have been there all along suddenly appear in your life. You 'luckily' hear about extra ways to make money, you 'coincidently' meet these people that are your perfect clients, you 'quite by accident' hear about your perfect job, because that information has been allowed through that filter and your conscious mind now becomes aware of these things that were there all along.

It's all a matter of programming, or training your subconscious in what IS important. That's why a lot of the exercises you discover throughout this book are so beneficial to you, because you're learning how to program your subconscious with what you DO want to bring into your world. All those things you desire are there all the time, but right now you're filtering them out. So the exercises I give you, the more you do them, the more they are programmed in. Repetition can be the key here, the more you do something, the more it is ingrained in the subconscious.

There is also an easy way to open that filter and program your subconscious…

You can open the RAS quite easily by getting into what is called an Alpha State. The energy in your brain is like electricity and the activity it generates are called Brain Waves. Scientists have found there are seven types of brain waves. The most common known are as follows:

◇ **Delta state** – when you are in a very deep sleep.

◇ **Theta state** – still asleep, but mostly dreaming, you're very relaxed; you can also access this state when you're in meditation.

◇ **Alpha state** – you're awake, but relatively quiet, the gateway between left and right brain is open, you're in what is called the 'whole brain' learning state.

◇ **Beta state** – when you are wide-awake where you can think of many things at once. Beta is where you also experience stress, tension, depression, self-doubts, and emotional outbursts. It's where you experience negative thinking. Beta is left brain driven. Spending your entire waking-life in Beta is like driving your car a thousand kilometres in first gear. You'll eventually get to your destination, but it will take an eternity, and you certainly won't enjoy the journey.

> *Picture your desires as a reality, and see them as already having occurred.*

The Alpha state is the one that allows you to attract your desires to you much more easily and quickly. The interesting thing is, since 1988 every country around the world has been training their Olympic Athletes using the Alpha state, so they can perform to the best of their ability and win gold medals. You can use this state to attract gold into YOUR life – **in the form of money!**

The Alpha state helps you remember easier, learn faster, create more and understand at a higher level. This is also known as the whole brain or peak learning state because you are tapping into both sides of your brain and any information you take in by-passes your short-term memory and goes directly to long-term memory. It amazes me teachers aren't shown how to take their students through a simple 2 minute exercise before each lesson. This would allow each child to access that peak learning state and achieve better results in the same time frame – maybe one day the Education Department will get up to date with the 21st Century (probably by the 22nd Century!)

You will begin to live the life of your dreams and attract wealth, riches and prosperity to you faster than you ever thought possible!

Alpha is the source of intuition, creativity and inspiration. The mind is free from the worries and frustrations of the physical world. You may unknowingly slip into Alpha when you're relaxing to gentle music, or when you're daydreaming. If you think back, you may realise you've often received answers, guidance and inspiration to help solve many of your problems, whilst you've been in that unintentional Alpha state. But now you'll be able to go there whenever you choose!

Beta is best described as 'head knowledge,' where you apply logic to everything you think, do or say. Alpha is best compared to 'heart knowledge.' **In Beta you 'think,' but in Alpha you 'know.'**

Your memory bank functions in Alpha. When you're in the Alpha state your memory is close to being photographic.

If you regularly go into the Alpha state, you can rejuvenate your body, enhance your natural healing power and pull energy to you quickly. Fifteen minutes in Alpha is equivalent to two hours sleep, so it's deeply relaxing, soothing and rejuvenating. In Alpha the left and right hemispheres of the brain are in balance, and working harmoniously together.

The easy way to get into that state is to slow your brain waves down. You can do this simply by taking the time to stop, get your body and brain quiet, close your eyes and take some deep breaths.

When you're relaxing your body, relaxing your mind and your breathing and brain waves slow down, you move into that Alpha state and that gateway opens. You can then think about the things you want to create in your life, picture your desires as a reality and see them as already having occurred. This is a powerful time to create. And guess what – <u>you are naturally in that state at least twice a day without even trying!</u> Those times are just as you are going to sleep and just as you are waking up. Use that special time to create the life of your dreams. Use that time to feed to your subconscious what IS important in your life, don't waste it thinking about what bills you have to pay and how .you have to go shopping and pick up Johnny from the dentist and the dozen other things on your 'to do' list.

<u>Make the time you go to sleep and wake up your creation time</u> – use it wisely and you will begin to live the life of your dreams and **attract wealth, riches and prosperity to you faster than you ever thought possible!**

 Wildly Wealthy Action Tip

Get into the Alpha state and think, feel and see your desires as already in your life!

Your Treasure Chest

'Star light, star bright... first star I see tonight...
I wish I may... I wish I might...
have the wish I wish tonight.'

ANON

As I mentioned earlier, as you drift off to sleep and as you are waking each day you are naturally in that <u>peak learning state, the Alpha state, where your subconscious and conscious minds are fully connected</u>. Use this powerful time to create your future. Use this time to think about your ideal life and **use this time to picture yourself as wealthy, rich, prosperous, successful and happy**. See yourself having already achieved your greatest desires; create an image of you living the life of your dreams; see that image, feel that image, walk into that image – don't just think about it in your mind, <u>experience it in your body</u>.

A great way to do this is to wait until you have been in bed for a few minutes and as you are lying there relaxed and at peace with your eyes closed ready to nod off for another night, **imagine at the end of your bed is a huge magical Treasure Chest**. You walk (in your mind's eye) to your treasure chest and slowly open the lid. You feel a sense of excitement as you realise this chest is filled with everything you desire. You slowly reach in and pull out your treasures. As you lovingly pick each one up, you <u>feel a sense of excitement and joy and unbridled happiness that you have been able to obtain your desires so easily</u>.

> *Picture yourself as wealthy, rich, prosperous, successful and happy.*

I recall when money was so tight, Christmas was coming and I was warning the kids that they wouldn't be getting many presents. They'd heard that before, but I had usually managed to 'pull the rabbit out of the hat' (and just go further into debt) because I didn't want them to go without. This year I was determined. I had made the decision that, no matter what, I was committed to getting out of debt. I was not going to blow any money that did come to me on presents that would be forgotten in a few months. I was keeping EVERYTHING to pay off my debts. **I was serious; I was on a mission; I was heading for financial freedom and nothing was going to stop me.**

As I drifted off to sleep each night, my Treasure Chest opened. Because I wanted to pay off my debts and didn't actually want 'things', I would just imagine money beginning to float out of the chest, slowly at first; a few $10 notes, then $20s then $50s then those beautiful $100 notes. As I watched in fascination, notes of all colours (Australian money is like a rainbow!) would fly out of the chest, up to the ceiling and then float down into my room. I could see the money flowing

When you add the emotions in your heart, it will make you magnetic to your desire.

to me; blue notes, red notes, purples notes, orange notes and my favourite, the big green notes. I could feel how liberating it was to have so much money, knowing that it was MORE than I could ever hope to spend. I felt unburdened, light, expansive, joyous, excited, relieved and grateful. I would watch the money continue to fall into my room until it either filled the room totally, or I fell asleep.

About a week before Christmas I dropped into the Post Office to collect my mail. There is something about receiving letters that I have always loved, but at that time, a part of me still dreaded getting the mail in case there was an outstanding bill. An official looking letter from a financial firm make me feel sick to the pit of my stomach. "Don't let it be one of those collection notices" I thought with dread. I ripped it open and stared in disbelief. Inside was a card from one of my ex-husband's old footballer friends – and a cheque for $5000. The card explained that when he'd borrowed the money from my ex (about 8 years earlier) he'd been told to send the repayment to me.

I just broke down crying right there at the Post Office. I couldn't believe my eyes! **The Universe works in the most amazing ways** – my ex, who had become very wealthy since we parted, had zero compassion for my current circumstances (which was a blessing in disguise as I was driven to create my own financial fortune!). Although he was paying the kids' school and medical fees, he was only contributing around $100 a month in child support to help with their daily expenses, and steadfastly refused to offer any more financially – and here was the Universe sending me this huge cheque that should have gone to him!

> *Get excited, and know that you are, in that moment, attracting your desires into your life.*

I was filled with an amazing mix of emotions – gratitude for getting the cheque, disbelief that I had so much money in my hands, fear that if I let my ex know I'd received the cheque he might actually make me give it to him (which, thank god, he didn't), and joy at knowing I could pay off some of those 'red letter bills'. After I dried my eyes, **I did a little happy dance, and thanked the Universe all the way home!**

Needless to say, I stood by my promise and only used a tiny amount to buy the kids a Christmas present, and used most of the money to pay off my bills. I use this technique on a consistent basis; it's easy, it's fun and it sure is a lovely way to drift off into dreamland!

Take a few moments each night as you go to sleep and as you awake each morning to focus on your desire and create the picture in your mind. <u>When you add the emotions in your heart, it will make you magnetic to your desire.</u> This is also a great 'game' to teach your children. Ask them to picture in great detail all their 'treasures' coming out of the chest and tell them to feel the excitement as they play with or use each one. It helps them to focus on what they would like to create in their life and is particularly good with younger children who feel a little afraid going to sleep at night. It encourages them to focus on wonderful, fun things, rather than that scary monster under the bed!

Your Treasure Chest exercise can be as detailed or as simple as you like. <u>The main thing is to keep it fun</u> – feel what it's like to be a child at Christmas time again and experience the emotions in your body as you take your own treasures from your chest. **Get excited, and know that you are, in that moment, attracting your desires into your life**.

 Wildly Wealthy Action Tip

Open your Treasure Chest every night as you drift off to sleep and feel the joy of owning all your treasures.

Go to <u>www.WildlyWealthy.com</u> to find out more about the powerful Prosperity Desires of the Heart visualization.

Brain Food for
Poverty or Prosperity?

"Life is a grindstone, and whether it grinds you down or polishes you up is for you and you alone to decide."
CAVETT ROBERT

One of the reasons I advise against watching a lot of TV is because **guess what state you are naturally in when plonked in front of the idiot box,** relaxed, breathing deeply, and generally 'zoned out'?? That's right, the Alpha state. And guess what state your children are in when they are watching TV shows full of violent, abusive, disrespectful and unlawful behaviour – again, the alpha state, the peak learning state.

So stop for a minute and think about what you want your children to create in their lives. How do you want your children's future to look? If you want their lives to be something more than what is experienced in the usual sitcoms or reality shows or drama or horror movies they watch week after week – then turn off the TV and feed them what you WOULD like to see them create in their lives. **If you can't do it for yourself, then at least do it for your children!**

I remember when I made the decision to 'disconnect' our family from the media. It actually worked out quite well, because we'd just moved house, and for some reason the antenna wasn't yet hooked up. So I made up some excuse about not being in a good area to be able to pick up stations, and we had to get someone special in to check it out. The first week was pretty dramatic – I think we all went through withdrawal symptoms. But as the weeks went by, I found the kids began to automatically look for other things to do. My daughter began to read everything in sight, going through big thick books in one weekend. My son played with his Lego, with his cars, with his toys and eventually they both stopped asking when the TV was going to work again. Mind you, they went to their Dad's every second weekend, so they got a bit of a TV fix (I'm sure they sat glued to it from Friday night until Sunday afternoon!)

We moved house again and even then the kids didn't ask about TV. The funny thing was, I had a friend who really wanted to watch the Melbourne Cup at my place. It's a special horseracing event that stops the whole of Australia the first Tuesday in November every year. People all over the country arrange special luncheons and fashion parades etc (really just another great excuse for a day off work!). One of my girlfriends came around and we ate strawberries and chocolate and watched the race and had a great time.

Remember how everything is vibrating, including your thoughts? Well guess who tapped into my thoughts that day? My daughter came home that night and said to me, "You know what, I really feel like watching TV, I just thought about it today and I really want the TV to work" and she turned it on and low and behold she was mesmerised – the TV was working once again!

There are many wonderful shows on TV; it's not all bad. Just don't watch them all in the one week! Be aware of not only what you are watching, but how much time you are spending focusing on other people's lives. Every minute in front of the TV is adding to your 'predominant mental attitude'. **Why not tip the scales in favour of wealth, and read out your affirmations, create a vision board or kiss some money?**

 Wildly Wealthy Action Tip

If you must have your TV fix, at least limit the time and choose shows that inspire, uplift and motivate!

Mastermind Your Way to Millions

'Keep away from people who try to belittle your ambitions
Small people do that,
but the really great make you feel that you too
can somehow become great.'
MARK TWAIN

In her book *The Dynamic Laws of Prosperity* Catherine Ponder talks about the increase in power when two or more people begin to focus on the same objective. In *Think and Grow Rich* Napoleon Hill talks about how powerful a Mastermind of people focused on the one outcome can be. You are already utilising the power of a Mastermind. It is best if you understand how it actually works.

When two or more people begin thinking about an objective in a harmonious way, there is more than just double mind power at work. When two or more people are focused, you find increased energy and ideas are released upon that desire, outcome or objective.

> *The Universe hears it all and then sends back to you what you've had your attention on the most.*

When two minds or more are blended towards a single purpose they tune in to a Higher Power that is filled with higher ideas and intelligence, which reveals to them the right way to proceed. In other words, **when two or more people are focused on the same idea, outcome, desire or objective – they tap into something far more powerful than each of them**

do alone; a synergy is created that enhances their thoughts, ideas and creative ability. The power multiplies – a Mastermind is at work.

A Mastermind can work to advance you OR (as often happens) to drag you down.

When friends get together it usually goes something like this: "Hi Mary, how're things going with you this week?" "Hi Sue, oh, not too bad. Although I got our electricity bill yesterday and I just about fell off my seat – it was $100 more than the last one". "Oh, you think that's bad; we had to get new tyres for our car and they cost nearly $700". "Really, that's terrible. Well guess what happened to Sally; she had a phone bill of almost $1000; seems her kids were phoning their friends' mobile phones". "You're joking! My gosh! Well I heard about this girl named Rosanna, and she blah, blah, blah"– and on it goes.

You not only bring your own experience into the conversation, you start dragging in the tragic stories of friends and their friends and then friends of friends and very soon you are focusing on **the financial woes of people you don't even know!**

You are creating a Mastermind. You are unleashing that amazing creative force – but what you're doing is creating MORE money challenges, MORE financial struggle, MORE bills and MORE woes for yourself!

When two or more people focus on the same objective, that creative

> *Utilise the power of a mastermind by connecting with a group of like-minded, positive people on a regular basis!*

force multiplies! By talking about the same things day after day with your friends, co-workers, family etc. you are repeating your order to the Universe **AND using the power of a Mastermind to speed up that order!**

The Universe is ALWAYS listening, not only when you talk about what you want, but also when you talk about what you don't want. The Universe does not judge if what you're 'asking' for is good or bad, it just picks up on your dominant vibration, your predominant mental attitude and accepts that as your order. **The Universe hears it all and then sends back to you what you've had your attention on the most.**

So be aware of the words you speak – **your words create your world** and when two or more people focus on the same objective, that creative force multiplies! As I've said many times already – focus only on what you DO want. Don't make the mistake of thinking 'focus' is only when you are deep in the alpha state and visualizing, or intently saying your affirmations and attaching emotion. **Any time you are thinking, listening or speaking you are 'focusing'.** Choose your thoughts wisely.

> *'Thoughts become things, choose the good ones'*
> Mike Dooley

It's also extremely beneficial if you utilise the power of a Mastermind by connecting with a group of like-minded, positive people on a regular basis. **You will amplify your requests through the synergy created** and find yourself embracing a life of prosperity and happiness far quicker than you would on your own – so begin Masterminding today!

 Wildly Wealthy Action Tips

Unleash a Mastermind to create good in your life.

Visit www.WildlyWealthy.com and join the Wildly Wealthy Mastermind.

Soar with the Eagles

'Success is not to be pursued,
it is to be attracted by the person you become.'
RICHARD CARLSON

It is a well known fact that we become what we think about all day long. It is also true that we attract friends into our life who are very similar to ourself. It is very important who you choose as friends; who you spend time with and who you are influenced by on a daily basis.

You are now aware that you become what you focus on consistently, and if you only spend time with friends who are struggling with money, always complaining about their situation, and always focusing on the negative, then what usually happens is you get together and commiserate with each other and compare your 'unpleasant financial situations' – **you are setting that powerful Mastermind force into action.**

If you want to create more prosperity and abundance in your life, you must surround yourself with people who are positive, who have great relationships and are creating wealth and success in their own lives. If you 'step up' your social and business circle, you 'step up' in your life too. You will set that positive Mastermind force into action.

Someone once said, "Hang with people who make you look bad". Well I had to stop and think about it for a second, it didn't make sense initially. "Why would I want to hang with people who make me look bad?" But think about it. If you hang with a group of people and you're the most successful, you make the most money, your life is so much better than theirs, sure it makes you look good, and it sure makes you feel good, but you **don't really have to push yourself** and it's very easy to get stuck in that same place.

Whereas, if you hang with people who 'have what you want', who are making things happen the way YOU want to make things happen in your own life, you will strive to do better. **You will move out of your comfort zone, you will try more, you will grow and challenge yourself, and you will achieve more and begin to see wonderful changes in your life**.

You will find that as you become more aware and your energy or vibration increases, destructive or negative people **will naturally move out of your circle and people who support the more evolved you will move into your circle**. You will naturally attract people into your life who encourage you and assist you to create the life of your dreams. You may also find one of the reasons your friends or family are negative towards you and your ideas to become more is, <u>they are afraid that you will change and leave them behind</u>. They may not be happy with the way their life is now, but change (in themselves and in others) can be very confronting and many are afraid to stretch beyond their comfort zone. Often people prefer to remain victims rather than take responsibility for their circumstances.

When your life begins to change, as you see more wealth flowing in, as you become more successful, you can share with your friends and family why things are improving, and what you are doing to achieve those results. **Those people who have a desire to improve their own life may begin to implement some of the same ideas (share this book with them!)** while those who are afraid to move out of their comfort zone will continue down the same path, maybe for the rest of their lives.

What I have learnt is this – when we are able to make enormous changes in our lives, we usually get an overwhelming desire to 'change the world' and help everyone within spitting distance to 'see the light' and improve their lot. <u>The thing you MUST remember is, people will only listen when they are ready to learn</u>. People will only take action when they are ready for change. People will only take any notice of you when they too are 'ready for something' (even if they don't know exactly what that something is). You simply cannot make others interested in something they are not ready for. You can share with them all the great techniques, ideas, tips and secrets within this book, but if they are not ready, it will be like water off a duck's back. You are basically wasting your time and theirs.

I have found the best approach is waiting. **If they ask you what you're doing, if they seem curious about the changes in your life, if they genuinely seem interested, then that is the time to share (or give them this book).**

And speaking from experience again, it is truly wonderful when your friends are ready to open up to a new way of thinking and they join you in your discussions of creating their future the way they want it to be. <u>It makes your time together so much more uplifting and exciting</u> than when you used to get together and just gossip and compare bad news stories.

Make the decision to be an eagle and soar to great heights.

 Wildly Wealthy Action Tips

Hang with people who are already where you want to be.

Share your life-changing information with those who are ready to listen.

See Your Dreams Into Reality

'What lies behind us, and what lies before us are tiny matters to what lies within us.'
RALPH WALDO EMERSON

The Universe desires you to have everything you want to have, the Universe is there to support you to Prosperity – The Universe is on your side! If you desire Riches, Wealth, Abundance and lots and lots of Money, <u>it's because the Universe wants you to have all those things, it supports you to have all those things, it is already devising plans and putting into action the steps necessary for you to have all those things</u>. Visualization, or creating pictures in your mind, will propel the riches you desire into your life at a rapid rate!

To put it simply, what you see is what you get. Visualization is the ability to use your imagination to see images in your mind. **When you add concentration and feelings, it becomes a great creative power that makes things happen.** Used in the right way, visualization can bring life-changing transformation into your life. The initial thought is the matrix — the blueprint — the plan; the feelings

> *Visualization, or creating pictures in your mind, will propel the riches you desire into your life at a rapid rate!*

provide the energy — the electricity — the power to make it happen. Visualization is an amazing tool; it enables you to experience your desires on a whole different dimension. It assists you to design a life bigger and better than you are currently living and enables you to create true prosperity! <u>And the best part is – it's easy and a whole lot of fun!</u>

The Power of Creative Visualization is a tried and true technique that helps you create the life you want. Creative Visualization is the art of communication on the visual level between your conscious and subconscious minds. Use your imagination and see images in your mind, then... when you charge these images with your concentrated thoughts and feelings you are commanding the creative power that makes things happen. The process of visualization is simple — yet this is more than closing your eyes and just picturing what you want; this is **designing your future and charging it with the energy required to attract your desires straight back into your life!**

You should visualize while you are deeply relaxed, as frequently as possible and as long as is convenient. Going into a meditative state isn't necessary. The most important thing is clarity and strong focus on what it is you desire, on what you want to attract into you life. For many, being intensely focussed suggests going into a meditative state, or even day-dreaming. The difference is that day-dreaming is usually an unplanned event that randomly occurs, whereas creative visualization is deliberate and goal oriented. Day-dreaming is hoping you will create or attract; visualization is the

> *Day-dreaming is hoping you will create or attract; visualization is the actual creation process.*

actual creation process. This is the kind of visualization that all top athletes in all sports and successful people in all areas of life will tell you they use. **They always see their success ahead of time.**

The first part of visualization is idealization. When you picture in your mind what you want, you are sowing the seed, but before sowing any seed it is desirable to know what the harvest will be. This is idealization. **Get clear on what you desire, so you can breathe life into it.**

Choose your desire, your dream or your goal carefully. Choose goals and desires that you feel extremely passionate and excited about. This powerful energy will infuse your vision with incredible life force which causes your desire to be created very quickly. **For**

rapid results it must be something that makes your soul stir and your heart sing; something you love to think about all the time. There are certain emotions that will energize your visualization so it will quickly manifest your desires. These are passion, love, joy, fun, light-heartedness and enthusiasm.

Love and Enthusiasm are particularly powerful attractors. The definition of enthusiasm is – 'inspiration as if by divine power'. People with the gift of enthusiasm carry a special kind of energy. Bringing enthusiasm to your visualizations means you are connecting your 'order' directly to that Universal source of all there is. You're tapping into the hotline!

This powerful energy will infuse your vision with incredible life force which causes your desire to be created very quickly.

When you visualize, you begin by making the mental image; make it clear, distinct and perfect. Hold that vision firmly in your mind. When you hold this picture firm, and energize it with positive emotions, the ways and means will develop, supply will follow the demand and you will be led to do the right thing at the right time and in the right way. **All sorts of amazing events you can't even imagine will unfold to bring you your desire**.

How do you get good at visualization so you can attract your desires into your life? Like anything, through practice. Start by visualizing things that you can already see around you. Pick an object, stare at it, and look at every detail. When you think you know exactly how it looks, close your eyes and re-create the picture in your mind. Visualizing should be fun. Even though all the techniques, secrets and exercises you learn within the pages of this book are very powerful, it is the energy behind them which is the most important piece of the puzzle, not so much the actual techniques.

To begin your visualization, find a place that is quiet and free of distractions. Take the phone off the hook and adjust the lighting as needed.

◇ Sit comfortably

◇ Close your eyes...relax your body, neck, shoulders, torso, head and jaw

◇ Relax your mind – clear your thoughts

◇ Take three slow, deep breaths – inhaling through your nose, relaxing, then exhaling slowly through your mouth

◇ Feel a wave of relaxation flowing through your body

◇ Now you're ready to begin...

Let's say your desire is for your dream home. See yourself walking along the road; you feel the wind in your hair and the sun on your face. As you walk, you see a beautiful home – your new home – feel the joy you feel through your body as you walk up to the front door and turn the key in the lock. You slowly open the door and take a step inside; what do you see? A smile crosses your lips as you look around and walk softly across the floor.

You notice the colour scheme and are thrilled with the way it looks. It's exactly as you pictured it would be. You walk past the kitchen and smell your favourite dish cooking in the oven – yummm – you're looking forward to dinner tonight. As you walk through the lounge and admire your beautiful furniture placed around the room you stoop to straighten the soft plump cushions on your comfy sofa. The floor covering under your feet feels luxurious and you slowly step outside to look around and breathe in the air. You feel the soft breeze on your face and stop for a moment to listen to the sounds in the distance. You are flooded with gratitude as you take in the expansive view.

Attracting what you desire isn't work – it's FUN!

From where you're standing, can you see the ocean, or the mountains, maybe for you it is a lush forest, or perhaps a cityscape? You feel excited and happy and so very proud of yourself for all you have achieved and you slowly turn and step back inside. You walk across the room and as you gently sink into your comfy lounge chair, you close your eyes and every fibre of your being shouts 'THANK YOU' to the Universe for making your dreams a reality.

This is an easy exercise. Once you have mastered the art of visualization, you will be able to easily pop into your own 'movie theatre' in your head any time you want. **Attracting what you desire isn't work – it's FUN**. It's about being a child again; it's about letting your imagination run wild. When you visualize, you see it as real. <u>Your subconscious doesn't know the difference between something that is real and something that is vividly imagined</u>. Use that to your advantage. Once your subconscious believes something is true (by repeated affirmation and/or visualization) it will do everything in its power to make sure you are aware of people, events and circumstances that WILL make your dream a reality.

Once you visualize what you desire you have begun a powerful process. Once you visualize your desire using as many of your senses as possible, it has the potential to manifest. **Once the visualization has been energised with emotion, the actual manifestation doesn't require any effort; it will happen automatically**. It really is that simple, it really is that easy.

So begin visualizing riches, abundance and wealth in your mind today, and watch them appear in your world!

 Wildly Wealthy Action Tip

Practise creative visualization daily.

Expand Your Prosperity Consciousness

'Let a man radically alter his thoughts,
and he will be astonished at the rapid transformation
it will effect in the material conditions of his life.'
JAMES ALLEN

As mentioned before, if you are going to attract more of anything into your life, you first have to expand your comfort zone around that thing you desire. <u>When it comes to attracting money, riches, wealth and abundance into your life, this is particularly so.</u> The last thing you want to do is master all these great techniques and find money flowing to you from all directions, only to see it flow out just as rapidly because you have not taken the time to move into a bigger, more expansive comfort zone around prosperity. The exercises and tips you are learning in this book enable you to feel more comfortable with larger and larger amounts of money.

Have you ever heard of Bikram Yoga? It's where you do a series of yoga asanas or postures, but in a room heated to body temperature. The idea behind the heated room is that your muscles will be more flexible from the start because they are already warmed, plus you have the additional benefit of releasing more toxins through the skin as you work up a sweat very quickly. I had already been practising the most wonderful 'power yoga' classes with an amazing teacher for about a year or so before I attended a Bikram class, so thought I would be just fine. Well, let me tell you – I was definitely outside my comfort zone.

Within the first 5 minutes of the class (we were still in the breathing exercise – how embarrassing) I had to stop because I thought I was going to faint. The heat was almost unbearable.

During the next 90 minutes I had to not only stop, but lie down on my yoga mat at least 15 times because I thought I was either going to faint or throw up. I left there vowing never to return. Unfortunately, I had paid for a special 3-session pass, and my frugal side would not let me waste the other two sessions, so I waited a couple of weeks to brace myself, and attempted another session.

To my surprise, I didn't feel nearly as wretched the second time – I only had to stop about five times. What had changed? Not the postures, they are the same week after week. Not the room temperature, it stays constant each session. The only thing that had changed was my comfort zone and my mindset. From just one yoga class to the next, I had moved from feeling like I was doing yoga in a sauna, to feeling like it was simply just uncomfortably hot. I had moved from absolute nausea and light-headedness to simply unpleasant. As I continued to go, it got easier and easier and the heat became quite OK. Nothing had changed about the sessions; I'd changed in my mind and my body.

> *There is a flood of abundance just waiting for you to claim it.*

It's **EXACTLY THE SAME** when it comes to your comfort zone around money, around riches, around having it all! Massive wealth is waiting for you to experience. It's right there for you all the time. There is a flood of abundance just waiting for you to claim it. You can go to the stream of prosperity with a teaspoon, or you can dip a cup in. You can choose to take a bucketful of wealth, or decide to jump right in and swim in that sea of abundance and prosperity.

<u>Your wealth is waiting for you always – the only thing that has to change for it to appear in your life is your comfort zone</u>. The only thing that has to change for you to claim it, is YOU. **Once you change who you are on the inside, there will be nothing stopping that wealth from flooding into your life on the outside.**

A wonderful, fun and easy way to expand your comfort zone around money is to become an instant Millionaire. Sounds like something you'd like to do? Well, you can practise spending your millions through playing the Millionaire Money Game. It's free and it's fun and all you need is an email address to participate. This powerful email game goes for eight weeks, and the basis of it is, I send you ever-increasing amounts of money, 'virtual money', that you get to 'spend' each day. All in all you will receive a few million dollars. You will be, day by day, little by little, expanding your comfort zone to accept more prosperity into your life. It's a game that brings an incredible energy and power to everyone who joins in the fun. We have thousands of participants from all corners of the globe each time we play. **You will be, day by day, opening yourself up to receiving more and more of what you DO desire into your life.** You tap into an amazing Mastermind and will begin opening yourself up to more prosperity in your life almost immediately!

Sign up now for The Millionaire Money Game and let the fun begin!

 Wildly Wealthy Action Tips

Consistently apply the Tips within this book to expand your Prosperity Consciousness.

Join the Millionaire Money Game to massively expand your comfort zone at www.millionairemoneygame.com.

Make More
Money NOW!

*'If your outgo exceeds your income,
then upkeep will be your downfall.'*
BILL EARLE

Never were truer words spoken than in the above quote. The only way to create long lasting wealth is to **bring in more than you spend** or **spend less than what you bring in**.

If your outgoing exceeds your income you are your own worst enemy on your path to creating a life of prosperity. <u>On a metaphysical level, you will be repelling abundance because you know that week after week you are going backwards, you are digging yourself deeper into a hole.</u> This will put up a force field stronger than any metaphysical actions you could possibly conjure up. This is when you have no choice but to do something practical. This is when you have to prove to the Universe you are now totally 100% committed to transforming your financial world and you are ready to have riches flow to you.

> *The only way to create long lasting wealth is to bring in more than you spend or spend less than you bring in!*

To turn the tide you have three choices – you may only need to use one to change your circumstances, but if you are really serious, you would be best to utilize two or, for increased attracting power, all three of the following steps.

1. <u>Increase the frequency of your metaphysical manifesting techniques</u> – continue to apply the techniques and the

exercises I have shared with you. Spend more time on the "being" so the money comes to you easily and effortlessly.

2. Look through the information from tracking your money and <u>choose to spend differently</u> (stop spending money in ways that may not be in your best interest).

3. <u>Increase your income</u> by including some practical steps to bring more money in e.g. Get a part-time job or start a home-based business (see further suggestions below).

As I said, for best results, you will need to use two or all three techniques. I remember doing the first two and still not quite getting ahead. The last thing I wanted to do was get a job, but I felt it was my only option. I felt it would show the Universe, without a shadow of a doubt, **that I would do whatever it takes to bring more money into my life.** I also knew that with a part-time job I would have a regular consistent income (when you have your own business, the money tends to flow fast and slow, and it can be frustrating going though a slow time).

When I began my job, although the money was not much, I knew it was coming in each week and it was additional money so I made sure it went directly into paying off debts. It wasn't used for extra treats or shopping sprees, it was to make me feel better about the money I owed, to lessen the burden and to free up my money energy. That's what I needed to turn things around. That may be all you need to turn things around.

I wasn't getting a job thinking it was my life-long career. **It was a short-term money-making option only**. It helped to free up the energy I held around money so more could flow to me. Within one month of starting part-time work I found I was building a new business with a direct sales company that allowed me to make a profit of $84,000 four short months later – that's $84,000 profit in that fourth month alone! It worked for me, and **it will work for you** too.

You've got to find what suits your circumstances. Obviously with a part-time job, it really doesn't matter what you end up doing. As long as it's legal and safe, then it shouldn't be a big deal. You're doing it to pay off some debts, or build a small nest egg to catapult you to the riches you deserve. **The intention behind your job is of utmost importance.** If you do something and <u>know with every fibre of your being that this is moving you closer to financial freedom, then that is what you will create</u>.

There are dozens of ways to bring more money into your life – even if you have a family and commitments. There are many things you can do that are flexible and can fit around your current schedule.

There are hundreds of part-time jobs that can bring you money immediately. Here are some suggestions:

◊ Waitress or Waiter

◊ House sitter

◊ Baby sitter

◊ Casual store assistant

◊ Night packer (at grocery store)

◊ Pizza delivery driver

◊ Typist for busy businesses

◊ Telemarketer

◊ Mystery shopper

◊ Commission salesperson

◊ Leaflet/pamphlet delivery

◊ Model

Once, when my daughter was around nine and going through the "I want to be a model" phase, I took her to a modelling agency. While I was there they asked if I wanted my son's picture on the 'Head Sheet' (the poster given to potential clients) as it wouldn't cost much more for two of them. "Why not?" I thought, thinking there probably wasn't much demand for six-year-old models.

Much to my surprise, a month later I got a phone call asking if he was available for a photo shoot for a new housing estate. They needed two photos, one of him eating breakfast with his 'model family', and one hanging from a tree smiling. The job was an hour's drive from where we lived, so I asked how much he'd be paid. My mind was made up in an instant when they said he'd get around $1000! It was an easy job, but he wasn't really impressed with modelling, so when we received another phone call a few months later for another job he told me to find out what he had to do – he was going to think about it! When I told him they said he would have to go fishing, and run with a dog through the grass, he was in! All in all he made around $1600 – which came in very handy at the time. (I borrowed it from him until my own money started to flow!)

There are dozens of ways to bring more money into your life – if you live in a tourist or seasonal area, you could get a job picking fruit or assisting one of the many businesses focused on the tourist market. I believe, if you really want a job you will be able to get one... and if a job is not for you – the next chapter will be!

 Wildly Wealthy Action Tip
Increase your income so you bring in more than you spend.

Do What You Love and the Money Will Flow

'Passion for life and for our work is a critical element
of success and abundance.
Passion is a virtually unstoppable, attitudinal force
that generates energy, creativity and productivity.
When you love what you do, it's difficult not to succeed.'
RICHARD CARLSON

Creating your own business can be extremely fulfilling, fun and profitable. Notice I said CAN be. Quite often, it can also be stressful, time consuming and frustrating. But you will never know unless you try, and I believe that once you find your passion, your true calling, it no longer seems like work. You do it because you love it!

I always advise my clients to <u>start up their own home-based business while still working at their current job</u> (if they have one). The reason being, you may get extremely enthusiastic and quit your job or close down your business to start your new venture. If you go from getting a regular pay cheque to suddenly relying on your own new business for income, you may self-sabotage. Even if your business has the potential to make you ten times what your job did, if it is not initially coming in consistently (which can be the case, particularly in the beginning stages of a business) you may begin to focus on the negatives: how will you be able to pay your bills; where will the money come for the rent; and how are you going to get the cash for your next car payment?

You may focus more on the lack you are experiencing, than on the abundance that is about to flow – **and what happens when you focus on lack?** That's right, **you create it**. I always find the best formula is, start a new part-time business around what you are already doing and keep building that business until you find you are making **MORE money than from your job for at least three months straight**. When that happens, **you will be ready mentally** to quit your job. Keep in mind, if it's achievable to continue to build your business AND work at your job, you will be bringing in two lots of income. <u>Having multiple streams of income is the way to get ahead</u>, **the more money streams flowing to you, the faster you will be swimming in an ocean of plenty, and if one stream dries up – it's not big deal!!**

Here's a list of things you may be able to do as your own small business:

◊ Clean houses

◊ Do shopping for others

◊ Run errands for busy people

◊ Organise people's filing

◊ Do gardening

◊ Be a professional organiser - clear others' clutter

◊ Wash cars

◊ Walk dogs

◊ Virtual Assistant (like a PA, but run from your own home)

◊ Cook meals

◊ Pet sitting

◊ Clothing alterations

◊ Internet business

If you are good at sales, you could try a direct sales business. Even if you're not – anyone can learn to sell. **A networking or direct sales business can be very lucrative and if you find a**

product that is in demand, your income potential is unlimited! Believe me, I used to have a real block around sales; I felt very uncomfortable selling anyone anything, particularly if I was going to make money from it. In fact, I had such a block, <u>I wouldn't even work in my own Swimwear stores</u>. Then when I discovered the company marketing personal development courses and seminars and I loved the product so much I decided I had to give it a go (plus, some of the high income earners in the company were making multiple six figure incomes in one year – I wanted some of that!).

When I first began I felt sick – and I don't mean that figuratively, I mean that physically. **I actually felt so nervous that I thought I was going to throw up!** I am quite shy (although I am a master of disguise, most people would have no idea) and so having to interact with people I didn't know on a regular basis was not a comfortable experience for me. The fear of rejection in sales is the number one reason people give up. If you try to remember they are not rejecting you personally, they just aren't in the market for what you have to sell right now, it makes the rejection a little less personal, and therefore a little less painful. But like anything, **if you do something often enough you get used to it.** I not only got used to it, I became one of the top sales people in the country for them. <u>So don't ever tell me you can't sell, because if I could learn to be good at it</u> – **anyone can!**

The more money streams flowing to you, the faster you will be swimming in an ocean of plenty!

If you're creative in any way, you could also make extra money doing some of the following:

◊ Freelance photography

◊ Sell your own crafts at Sunday markets

◊ Freelance journalism

◊ Write an e-book and sell it on-line

◊ Design websites

◊ Create clothing or crafts and sell to stores

◊ Invent something

◊ Teach Teleclasses (find out more at www.teleclass.com or www.teleclassinternational.com)

◊ Become a Life Coach

◊ Sell your expertise; consulting, book reports, coaching etc.

◊ Start a networking/direct sales business (find my recommendations at www.WildlyWealthy.com)

If you really want to make good money, you could begin Real Estate investing to create a passive income – for life! At first this may seem quite daunting; you may even think you need a lot of money to do so. Well, guess what – you don't. In fact, once you learn how it is done, you can even invest in Real Estate with NO MONEY. Sounds crazy, but it's true.

Actually, the very first investment property I signed a contract on required not a single cent from me. I'd found a great deal, then I found a joint venture partner (who could finance the project) who was looking for a great deal. They had the money to put up as a deposit, and the ability to get a loan for the property. The deal was, we would split the income from the rent 50/50 and it didn't cost me a thing! You would be amazed at how many people have a lot of money and would love to invest in real estate, but simply don't have the time to find good deals. That's where you come in.

Also, once you know what type of properties people are looking for, you can find a piece of Real Estate for them and they could pay you a finders fee (quite often around $1000), or even do a joint venture like I did. This strategy works particularly well if you are part of a property investing network. There are many great seminars, courses and books that can teach you about Real Estate; go to the best (I'm just a **little biased**!) for more information on creating your own   financial freedom through Real Estate Investing and multiple streams of income visit: www.WildlyWealthyWomen.com. You can get a free information audio to find out more and discover if Wildly Wealthy Women is for you!

Starting your own business can be fun and is really quite simple. The thing to keep in mind about your part-time job is, it's usually a short term thing, you don't have to love it, it's easy to get out of at any time and it won't cost you anything to get started. <u>Your own business is another matter</u>. The trick is – **find something you love**. I am a busy person and have been known to be most unorganised (even I am surprised at what I have created in my life with this character flaw!) To keep my chaos under control, I occasionally get someone in to organize my clutter. I hate the clutter, but I also don't like cleaning it up, or to put it more exactly, <u>I would much rather be writing, creating, doing what I love to do</u>, than filing and sorting! And the thing is, whatever you don't like doing, someone out there LOVES doing it; it's what they are naturally good at; it's their passion.

You have to find YOUR passion. Once you do, let your enthusiasm sell your product or service. Visualize yourself as a great success, write a Desire Statement (you'll learn this in the next chapter) around your business and feel yourself experiencing the success you desire. Write an affirmation about the high profits you make each week or month. See it, feel it, enjoy it; be grateful for it. Believe me, this works so much better than writing out a Business Plan – and is a heap more fun too! When you do what you love, you create an amazing energy around you **that guarantees you will draw success, money and love to you in avalanches!**

Believe me, there is **always a way to make money doing what you love**. Before I even knew about the Law of Attraction I was finding many ways to make money with my passions.

I loved reading – I got a job in a library. One of my main jobs was to cover books; I got so good at covering books that I could cover them without looking – this allowed me to read at the same time. What fun!

Exercise was also a passion and I became an Aerobics Instructor. I held exercise classes which kept me fit and made me a lot of money at the same time.

As an aerobics instructor, I had a lot of spare time on my hands. I loved being down by **the ocean** so I ended up getting a morning job spraying people with suntan lotion and hiring out umbrellas at the beach. What a great job, sitting in a deck chair and getting paid for it!

I didn't watch much TV and liked to keep moving, so **night packing** at the local grocery store, which is very physical, was perfect. I didn't start until about 6.00pm and finished around 10pm. Again I was getting paid to keep fit!

Even now, I'm making an income from my passion. I teach others how to be wildly wealthy through my Prosperity Mentoring via Teleconference, Workshops and live

> *Believe me, when you are doing something you absolutely love and you're making money at the same time – it really doesn't get any better than that.*

Seminars all around the world and it doesn't seem like work at all; it's what I LOVE to do. Visit www.WildlyWealthy.com to find out more and discover lots of free prosperity resources.

I have also expanded my Millionaire Mindset workshops into a powerful Mentoring Program for women only – see www.WildlyWealthyWomen.com for details. My passion is studying Prosperity and the Metaphysical and sharing it with others. I get to do that with people from all around the world. **Believe me, when you are doing something you absolutely love and you're making money at the same time –** it really doesn't get any better than that!

Think about some of the things that you love to do, <u>things that you would do even if you weren't getting paid for it</u>. Make a list of things that interest you and then mastermind how you can turn that into a money making venture – either by working for someone else, or starting your own business. You would be surprised at how your passion can become your business and make you money – **more money than you ever imagined!**

List your passions, interests and strengths.

1. _____

2. _____

3. _____

4. _____

5. _____

6. _____

7. _____

8. _____

9. _____

10. _____

11. _____

12. _____

Wildly Wealthy Action Tips

Start your own business.

Visit <u>www.WildlyWealthy.com</u> for more great money-making ideas and to find out more about Wildly Wealthy Women.

State Your Desires

*'I suggest that if you firmly imprint your expectations
onto the Universe your yellow brick road will appear
in front of you, as if by magic.'*
SIMON HALL

As you should have gathered by now, it's all about focus; it's all about thinking mainly about what you DO want to attract in your life, rather than what you DON'T want to attract. You now have many tips, secrets and strategies you can use to change your focus so you become a magnet to all things prosperous.

'Desire statements' can be a great help to keep you focused. You can write these statements for any area of your life. I have used them for my physical health, for relationships, businesses and finances. Basically, **a Desire Statement is a one or two page outline of how you would like something to be;** <u>how the perfect outcome would look and what your ultimate scenario is</u>.

For instance – about four years ago I was attending an Anthony Robbins Seminar when they mentioned they were looking for additional coaches to work with them on a part-time basis from home – "Go and see our Trainer in the break if you want to know more". Well, I like to know everything, so along I went. Even though they did not actually need any Australian coaches, I decided that would be a great way to make additional money. Actually, I didn't really understand what a coach was, but I thought I could easily learn, and then I would have an additional stream of income.

When I returned to Australia, I attended a three day seminar for the personal development company I was working with. The English facilitator of the seminar, Marian Durrands, just happened to be in Australia with the idea of starting a Coaching Company. Her Coaching Company was just a concept at this time, although she seemed to think it would be up and running within the next few months. I thought that was a bit ambitious (I obviously didn't know Marian had a determination equal to mine!) and set about researching Coaching Academies on the internet.

I was surprised about eight weeks later to receive an invitation to an information evening as Marian's 'Life Coaching Academy' was ready to begin here in Australia. I happily went along to find out more and at the end of the night eagerly signed up to be part of the very first intake of students into the Academy. Mind you, I had to borrow the money to do so (yes, more debt to bury myself in) – but I just felt this was something I had to do.

After completing the residential weekend, I came away with everything I needed to get me going as a Life Coach – except clients and the confidence to make it happen. I already knew the power of writing something down, so I decided to be very specific around this one topic.

Now keep in mind, when I wrote this out, I had only attended a three day training weekend. I had zero idea about HOW I would be able to build a coaching practice, although <u>I did know the Universe takes care of the hows, if you just know WHAT it is you want</u>.

So I wrote this out (this is actually my original draft which I was going to revise and 'polish up' but never got around to doing).

Coaching Desire Statement

My coaching practice is rapidly expanding – I now easily and effortlessly attract positive, easy-going, successful, motivated, fun people who want to move to the next level in their lives and are willing to do what it takes.

I work with at least 15 new clients each month from around the world coaching them toward their own individual successes.

They love my style of coaching and are thrilled with the results they are achieving since partnering with me. They happily refer their friends and business associates to me, and my business just keeps expanding. It gives me such a feeling of fulfilment and a sense of accomplishment when I see my clients achieving their goals.

I have been trained as a Life Coach Trainer, and regularly train new groups of Life Coaches around Australasia. I have completed my Corporate Coach Training and am in demand as a highly successful Corporate Coach and make in excess of $2000 a month per client.

It fills me with such pride to see how far my practice has progressed in such a short space of time, and my children and friends are excited with what I have achieved for myself. I am able to choose my own hours and retain the flexibility and freedom that I love so much.

I now effortlessly attract abundance into my life and warmly embrace the prosperity that flows towards me and surrounds me now. My business and savings are growing even as I sleep, and my investments are making my money rapidly multiply. I am swimming in a sea of money, surrounded by a flood of riches, and am at one with absolute abundance, plentiful prosperity, unlimited wealth and total financial freedom.

I AM AT ONE WITH
PROSPERITY AND ABUNDANCE NOW!!!

When I wrote this statement, as I said, I had NO IDEA how it would come to pass. But less than six months later I DID have an international coaching practice. **I had clients from the US, New Zealand, Canada, Australia, Hong Kong, France, England, Germany and Ireland** – and they DID love my style of coaching.

Within that 6 months I was also selected to be a Life Coach Trainer and had been sent to various places around Australia to train new groups of coaches. When I wrote I wanted to be a trainer, again, I had no idea how I would be able to do that, I just (once again) thought it would be a great additional stream of income!

<u>Within six months about 90% of everything I had written down had happened.</u> <u>It can be that easy.</u> <u>It can happen for you too!</u>

One of the things I had written down – about being a Corporate Coach – I ended up not doing. I actually acquired a few corporate clients but decided, soon after coaching them for a short while, that I really wanted to focus on teaching others how to attract prosperity and abundance into their lives. I decided Corporate Coaching really wasn't my focus. Often you can get so hung up on deciding what to include in your desire statements or affirmations or visualizations that you end up never actually choosing because you can't make a decision. **Well the great thing about attracting your desires into your life is, if you decide it's not really what you want when they get there, you can just visualize them straight back out!**

When you write your Desire Statement, you may want to include: the sort of people you'd like to work with; how often you want to work; how much money you want to make; how you feel now you're successful; what you're doing. Don't get your logical mind too involved in the process. If you want a better job or business, just put in the guidelines for what you want and let the Universe take care of the rest. You can be very involved and go into great detail, and the more the better, but if it's so long that you don't have time to read it, then that's defeating the purpose. So you may be better to do as I did and keep it brief; but really see it and feel it when you read it.

This is a particularly good exercise to do if you rely on sales for your income, or have your own business. You can be as specific as you like and include all the things that will help you to be a huge success. This works; it's worked for me and hundreds of my clients – it's easy, it's fun and it's fast. <u>You just have to do it!</u> The Universe is waiting to give you what you want – you just have to place your order!

 Wildly Wealthy Action Tip
Write your Desire Statement.

Perfection Before Prosperity?

'Whatever you can do, or dream you can... begin it.
Boldness has genius, power and magic in it.'
GOETHE

I remember having a burning desire to teach others all I had learnt about attracting prosperity. **The more I learnt, the more I wanted to share.** It was all-consuming, and in the end I would get my dear friend Tania around to my house once a week, sit her down on the lounge and spend an hour each time lecturing her on everything I had discovered over the previous week.

I had been learning about Universal Laws and particularly the Law of Attraction for a while. I had been having some great successes – but also some horrific failures. I now know that it was due to the 'default message' (stuck on poverty consciousness) running through my mind, but I felt I couldn't actually get out there and teach others until I was really wealthy myself. I was working with a money coach at the time who said to me, "What are you waiting for? You think you have to be a millionaire before you can teach others but you only have to be further ahead of the people you are teaching. Just get out there and do it". And so I did. I am so glad I listened to her, instead of waiting forever for everything to be perfect. I just got out there and did it!

Coaching people around the world on how to attract even more prosperity and riches into their lives is something I've been doing now for years. Over that time I have had my ups and downs when it comes to creating my own wealth. I have overcome my poverty consciousness background and created a life so much richer, not just financially, but spiritually, than I could have imagined. **I absolutely LOVE what I do**. Visit www.WildlyWealthy.com to find out more.

I am a learning junkie – particularly around creating Abundance and Prosperity. I am forever reading, studying, finding new information, and then taking all that I learn and turning it into an understandable and useable format, so that people actually get results.

The ironic part was, even after I had been teaching my Millionaire Mindset program for around a year, I was still throwing my hands up in disgust. I used to wonder what on earth I was doing wrong. What was wrong with me? **Here I was, teaching others how to create a life of riches and wealth, but I was STILL struggling**. Most of my students were attracting all sorts of wonderful things into their life (as I often was) but I felt like I was on a roller coaster. I'd be going up, up, up to 'Wealth City' and then the next moment, I was going downhill fast. Then up, up, up again, only to plummet down into the depths of "Poor Ville" once more.

Whilst at the time it seemed incredibly frustrating and downright annoying, in hindsight it was the best thing that could have ever happened to me. Imagine for a moment that I had come from my money challenged background, begun to apply these same secrets I am now teaching you, and then had instant success. I am sure if I had then shared my message I would have affected quite a lot of people – particularly the ones who were also blessed enough to have instant success. But all those people who were a bit slower to create the wealth they desired, all the ones who struggled, all the ones who needed more time and energy to attract true prosperity, just like me, would have given up. But that is now the MAIN thing I teach – never, never, never give up. Never say, "This works for everyone else, but it won't work for me". **Never think that everyone else has the ability to become rich beyond their wildest dreams, but the Universe has singled you out to live a life of poverty**. Because I know that if it can work for me, if I can totally transform my finances and create the life of my dreams – then YOU CAN TOO!

It just takes some of us a little longer to become rich. It takes persistence; it takes practice; it takes consistent effort and it takes diligence. The thing is, we are all human, and it's human nature to want a result and to want it now. But it's also human nature to be lazy, and to expect to get results without too much effort. Even though I was teaching these principles to others around the world, I wasn't always practising what I was preaching; and it wasn't until I was practising them on a daily basis that things really began to take a turn for the better.

The lesson I have learnt is, as long as you do something every day, then you will, little by little begin to tap into that flow of abundance. And once you begin to see signs of even a little bit more prosperity, you will begin to believe that maybe, just maybe, it's starting to work for you. And **once you begin to have that belief, then you will begin to attract even more prosperity and then your belief will grow, then you will attract even more and on and on it goes**.

If I had waited until I was a millionaire before teaching others, it would probably have never happened. If I had waited until I was rich beyond my wildest dreams, I probably would never have experienced the riches I do now. I listened to my coach's words and then remembered back to a swimming teacher I once had. She was the best in the state; many of her students were champions because she was such a good instructor. She would pace up and down the pool, shouting instructions, urging her protégées on. I once asked Mum why she never actually got into the pool with the kids she taught. The answer shocked me. "Because she can't swim" she said.

> *As long as you do something every day, then you will, little by little begin to tap into that flow of abundance.*

Some people are destined for greatness through teaching others, but not actually experiencing it themselves. For a while I thought that was the case for me and money. There is nothing that could hold me back from teaching others how to create a life of wealth and abundance. I have to share – it is my passion. At one stage, I just thought maybe I was not destined to live a prosperous life. **Thank Goodness the Universe had other plans**! I was just being challenged; I was being tested; I was being put through the wringer so that thousands of others would then benefit from my experiences.

Sometimes you have to take that leap of faith; you have to just commit; you have to prove to the Universe that THIS IS IT. You won't take it any more, you've had enough and it's time for the Universe to pay up!

I remember finishing one of my Millionaire Mindset sessions and feeling so down-hearted that my students were really making it happen and here I was with another bill I couldn't pay. I sat on my bed and screamed at the Universe, "Show Me The Money". Not knowing what to do next, I decided to clean out my cupboards and slid the door closest to me open. I picked up a pile of magazines and underneath was one of my photocopied

> *The Universe wants you to be Wildly Wealthy beyond anything you have ever experienced before!*

hundred dollar notes – or so I thought until I turned it over and it wasn't just white paper on the other side – it was real! **I was instantly $100 richer and thanked the Universe profusely.**

The Universe is always listening, but sometimes we have to scream with every ounce of emotion we have for it to speed up our abundance. Always remind yourself that prosperity is coming to you just as surely as it came to me. Your flood is on its way, because if you don't give up, the Universe doesn't give up – it's guaranteed. The Universe wants you to be Wildly Wealthy beyond anything you have ever experienced before!

 Wildly Wealthy Action Tip

Continue, persist, keep going, and your abundance WILL appear.

Now You See It, Now You Don't

'When you affirm big, believe big and pray big, big things happen.'
NORMAN VINCENT PEALE

The road to a life filled with abundance can often be a rocky one with many twists and turns. Sometimes it can seem easier to stay where you are, deep within your comfort zone, than to venture out to new uncharted territory, where you could become Wildly Wealthy!

You too may experience the ups and downs I did when it came to money. You may create wealth, only to lose it. You may tap into the flow of abundance, only to see it dry up once again. Don't despair. Just know the prosperity you desire is ALWAYS there. Your riches are always waiting for you, always surrounding you. **Sometimes the cash isn't there because you are still expanding your comfort zone around money and you push away (on a subconscious level) the money that is beyond what you are used to**.

And sometimes the money isn't there because you choose to think it's not coming. And remember, what you think, what you believe, what you speak, is what you end up creating.

I have learnt a valuable lesson. Sometimes life does not go the way you planned. Full stop. End of lesson. The thing is, when it doesn't go the way you would have preferred, you have two choices. One is to go with the flow, accept it and move on. **The other is to get annoyed, feel angry, rant and rave about how unfair it is and focus on it so much that you re-create it again and again in your life**.

Are you re-creating challenges, dramas and bad luck over and over in your life by focusing on it, thinking about it, analyzing it, phoning your friends and telling them about it? **Let it go and move**

on. Re-create a new and empowered future by letting go of the past – today!

You have to face the responsibility of where you are in your life right now. You can no longer blame your past, your present or your future, your family, your friends, your job, your boss, the economy, your age, your weight, your knowledge, your location, your health or anything else in the entire world. Everything that has occurred in your life is because YOU thought it first, maybe consciously, maybe subconsciously. Maybe you were just focusing so much on what you didn't want, that you attracted it right into your life. It doesn't matter any longer. You know the secret to living the life of your dreams; just keep focusing on what you do want and **persist, don't give up, no matter what happens** and it will be yours!

> *Just keep focusing on what you do want and persist, don't give up, no matter what happens and it will be yours.*

I love to travel to the U.S. and have done so many, many times in the past few years. Being the queen of frugal, I still travel economy, but always request an exit row seat because of the extra room. When you're flying for around fourteen hours straight, it's nice to be able to stretch your legs without bumping into the seat in front of you, or be able to go to the ladies without having to wake the entire row. I remember booking my seat and requesting my usual exit row only to be told, "Sorry, they're all taken". Because the plane was so full, I was told I would be right down the back of the aircraft – not a good sign, I get a little squeamish in the tummy the further toward the back I am. It may just be my imagination, but it seems the plane gets bouncier the closer to the tail you get.

I always try to be the last person to board; I prefer to spend as little time as possible on the plane. So as I made my way further and further down the aircraft, I noticed three empty seats in the exit row. Considering I was probably the last one on, I assumed they were empty and asked the flight attendant if I could wait there, and if no-one showed up, could I sit there. "Sure", she said. So I perched myself on the end of the seat and waited.

I'd only been there about thirty seconds when an older male flight attendant approached me and said "Show me your ticket please". Feeling a little guilty about my move (I know they don't like it when you play musical chairs) I told him this wasn't actually my seat and I was just waiting to see if it was free. He glanced at my ticket and said "Come with me please". I pleaded with him to let me stay put because I really wanted those seats, but he said to me curtly "Don't be silly, come with me". I thought he was going to take me to the back of the plane where my real seat was, but he turned around and marched toward the front. "We've got to look after our special clients", he said as he pointed to two empty business class seats and asked me to sit down. At this point I had no idea who he thought I was (me, dressed in my special 'long haul flying uniform' of tracksuit pants, running shoes, warm comfy jacket, backpack and no make-up) but happily sat myself down.

I'd only been there about sixty seconds when another flight attendant approached my seat and asked "Can I see your boarding pass please?" Feeling rather embarrassed, I explained that this wasn't actually my seat but the other flight attendant had said I should sit there. "You'll have to move, because these people have just boarded". I don't know where these passengers were hiding, because it looked as though I had definitely been the last to board. Oh well, I thought, that was fun while it lasted. And I got up and headed toward the back of the plane.

As I was walking back to my original seat, the older male attendant saw me and asked what I was doing. I explained about the two passengers and he muttered something under his breath and said, "Come with me". He then marched me back up to business class, found another empty seat and, knowing there couldn't possibly be any more people boarding at this late hour said, "You'll be fine here". Once again I happily settled in my seat. I stored my backpack, put my water bottle in the pocket in front, read through the dinner menu and chose the movies I would watch. I had a chat to the passenger to my side and generally felt extremely grateful and excited at being upgraded for no good reason!

Suddenly, another flight attendant asked for my boarding pass – **oh no, another last minute passenger taking MY seat**! How embarrassing. By now the whole of business class had watched me jump from seat to seat, probably thinking I was trying to scam my way into an upgrade. This time it was even worse because I had to re-pack my things and tidy up my space before I once again made my way down to the back of the plane. As I reappeared through the curtains and marched back into economy (with the entire plane staring at me) I once again met the older flight attendant. He took one look at me and almost exploded – he wanted to know why I was heading back down to the rear of the plane. I explained what had happened and by this time he was mumbling and grumbling about "not being happy about this." He gently grabbed me by the arm and marched me up to business class. When we got there, we just kept going, we walked straight through the next set of curtains and he turned to a huge comfy FIRST CLASS seat and said, "There, you're staying here for the rest of the flight". He gave me a smile and a wink and disappeared.

And let me tell you, I had the BEST flight I have ever had. I love flying with Qantas anytime, but this time was really something special. First Class is something I've always wanted to do and it was SO MUCH FUN with incredible food, wonderful service, and absolute comfort – definitely more my style than "cattle class". The interesting thing about this experience was that first I didn't have, then I did have, then I didn't have again, then I did have again, then I didn't have once more, then I had MORE than ever! At any time I could have done what most people would do, and focused on how I missed out, came so close and had it all taken away, but instead, I focused on how lucky I was to have – even for that brief moment. "How cool," I thought, "this is evidence that even bigger and better things are coming my way". And because I held that belief, that faith that more was on its way (even as I was marching to the back of the plane), **the Universe had no choice but to deliver**. And deliver it did – even bigger and better than I could have ever imagined!

So when you begin to tap into your wealth, when it begins to flow to you and then, for whatever reason, it disappears, don't focus on how you don't have it any more, <u>focus on how you did have it,</u> <u>and how that is evidence that you already know how to attract</u> <u>wealth</u>. Focus on how much fun it was, even if it was a brief moment, (and even if it was only a tiny piece of prosperity) and you will surely attract even more to you, because **the Universe can hardly** **wait to give you all you desire and then some!**

Also, don't get stuck in the twilight zone – where you think about what you desire half the time, and what you don't want the other half. If you think about prosperity and riches and wealth, and then worry about how you will pay your bills – the universe isn't clear on what to send you, so you may get a little of both, (a bit of money coming in, then more bills coming in) or you may get more of one than the other; a little bit of money and a LOT of bills - **especially if you** **worry MORE about your debts** **than get excited about being rich!**

The Universe can hardly *wait to give you all you* *desire and then some.*

Everything in your world is there because you thought of it, change your thoughts to total prosperity, abundance, wealth and riches ALL the time, and it is a scientific fact, **<u>you will begin to</u>** **<u>experience total prosperity, abundance, wealth and riches ALL</u>** **<u>THE TIME</u>**!! It has to happen; there can be no other outcome! This is science based on Universal Law, and if one person gets rich from it, then it is a fact that YOU too can get rich.

By the way, I never did find out who the Flight Attendant thought I was – maybe with my Aussie accent he thought I was Elle McPherson! (hilarious laughter from the author!)

 Wildly Wealthy Action Tip

Recognize there may be ups and downs on the road to riches; **focus only on the ups.**

One Drop and the Flow Begins

*'Wealth consciousness is so much more than simply
having the ability to make money.
It's a mindset that involves seeing life, not as a struggle,
but as a magical adventure where our needs
are met with grace and ease.
Wealth consciousness is a state of mind,
a sense, not of believing but really knowing that
what we need is available to us.'*

RICHARD CARLSON

Do you often wish you could win the lottery? Do you dream of what you will do with your millions? Do you celebrate your little victories or only get excited when you dream of your big wins?

Too often it is easy to think a few million dollars from Lotto or your big business idea that hits a home run will solve all your problems once and for all. Nothing could be further from the truth.

For a moment, in your mind's eye, picture your current financial situation as a garden bed that is dry, shriveled and sadly drooping. Now think of those millions of dollars you want in your life as a fire hose. <u>If you turn that fire hose on those flowers you will blow them right out of the garden bed,</u> **they don't stand a chance – they'll be blasted to Timbuktu and beyond!** Whereas, if you take a little water to them, bit by bit, on a daily basis and give them strength and nurture them, they will grow and thrive and bloom and shoot seeds which will then continue to grow year after year after year for the rest of eternity.

It's the same with your prosperity. **Don't think becoming an instant millionaire is the only way to go.** Don't try and blow your financial life away with a few million in one hit, just focus on a continual flow, bit by bit, day by day. Celebrate those small wins, those little signs of abundance. **It's the daily flow that allows you to live your life as you choose, it's the continual attraction of money into your life that gives you <u>proof that more is always on the way</u>,** that total financial freedom is within your grasp.

Are you clear on what manifesting actually is? According to the dictionary, it means 'distinctly evident, to show plainly, to make appear'. I like to think that one day in the not too distant future, humankind's manifesting skills will be greatly enhanced. We may even be able to manifest or attract our desires into our life by blinking our eyes as in *I Dream of Jeannie*, by wiggling our nose like Samantha from *Bewitched*, or even, as Harry Potter does, by waving a wand.

You manifest on a daily basis already. **You attract into your life whatever you think about – the good AND the bad. Whether you are conscious of this or not**, <u>it is always working</u>. How clever are you at manifesting the seemingly insignificant things, like green lights or parking spaces? Do you routinely attract these things to you on a weekly or daily basis, without even really thinking about it? – they

> *The power you use to attract a parking space is the same power required to attract a million dollars – there is no difference.*

just happen. <u>Did you know it is no more difficult to manifest your million dollars than it is to manifest your parking space?</u> The power you use to attract a parking space is the same power required to attract a million dollars – there is no difference! It's all a matter of belief – YOUR belief. You think one is easy, and the other is difficult. **<u>Change your belief and you will change your world.</u>**

Belief is strengthened by practice. If you continue to be grateful and excited about your little manifestations, your belief will continue to grow. As your belief grows, you will get better and better at attracting what you want consciously. With a stronger and stronger belief, you will be able to attract more and more into your life. **You will continue to become a magnet for ALL the things you desire.**

I remember those few weeks when I was working in my newfound job. I love chocolate, especially when I'm bored. Sitting in that shop gave me an overpowering urge for chocolate – but I was trapped. I wasn't allowed to leave so I had to sit there and think about how much I would LOVE to be chewing on a yummy chocolate at that moment.

One day an hour or so passed and all I could think about was how I could get some chocolate; I could taste it, my mouth was even watering! Suddenly a customer appeared (one of the few) and began looking through the clothes racks, and I noticed she had a paper bag in her hand. She picked something out of the bag and popped it in her mouth. "What are you eating?" I enquired (I like to know everything!). "Chocolates, I just bought them at the new lolly shop down the road", she replied, "Would you like some?" "Would I ever!" I thought, "I've only been sitting here for the past hour thinking of nothing else"! And boy oh boy, was I a happy little vegemite, (an Aussie saying when you're pleased as punch) only another chocoholic could have any idea how blissful a piece of chocolate is to a self-confessed chocoholic! "Thank you, thank you, thank you" I said to her and the Universe. I told her how grateful I was for her gift as I popped one of those chocolates in my mouth. And when she left I did a little happy dance around the shop. Sitting in that jail, whoops, I meant shop, I realized that "I still had it" and **if I just gave that same energy and focus to creating the life of my dreams, instead of just chocolate, I would not have to sit there much longer!**

It's that easy; it's that simple. Learning how to manifest, or attract your desires into your life, is the same as riding a bike. **Once you know how, you have that skill forever and ever.** You may at times hit a rough patch in the road; you may slide on the gravel and skin your knees. You may even hit a pothole, or crash into the curb and do some major damage. But you will still always know how to ride that bike. Using the Law of Attraction in your life is exactly the same. Once you know how, you can ALWAYS do it. You may forget some days, you may attract all sorts of things you don't really want and wonder what on earth is going on in your life. But the bottom line is, if you have consciously focused on something and it has come to pass, whether big or small, then you know how to create the life of your dreams. You just have to <u>practise, practise, practise</u> – so you focus on and attract who you DO want, not focus on and attract what you DON'T want!

You have to acknowledge all that does flow into your life. It doesn't necessarily take a million dollars to live the life of your dreams and achieve financial freedom. Your flow of abundance could be as simple as receiving a discount on this item, an unexpected cheque for that service, a friend gives you something they no longer need but you have been desiring desperately. It's all about being clear on what it is you do want, and letting the details be handled by the Universe, knowing that <u>it has a gazillion ways it can deliver your order</u>.

Understanding that the way for the flow to come is not only the fire hose of millions, but that continual flow day by day by day, so that all your needs are met, all your desires appear, all your dreams come true. Remember, a mighty oak began as an acorn, a tornado started as a breath of air, every Millionaire starts with their very first cent. Your flood of riches will begin as a trickle – acknowledge your trickle, get excited about your trickle, be grateful for your trickle – **<u>it is the beginning of a sea of plenty that you will be able to swim in for the rest of your days</u>**!

As you practise attracting what you desire into your life, there will be times when you feel like 'the golden child', 'the blessed one'. You will almost believe you have that magic wand and whatever you desire is merely a wave in the air away. And then there will be days when you feel as if you have flushed that wand down the toilet. Don't worry. Experience those down days and just let them go. Focus on what you DO want. The Universe is poised, ready to shower you with abundance and prosperity and wealth. **Keep your focus and the Universe WILL deliver!**

 Wildly Wealthy Action Tip

Acknowledge the prosperity flow, little by little – it is the beginning of your flood.

Open Yourself to Receive

'To believe in the things you can see and touch is no belief at all;
but to believe in the unseen is a triumph and a blessing.'
ABRAHAM LINCOLN

If you are applying all you learn but not yet seeing any increased prosperity in your life <u>you may be missing an important piece of the puzzle.</u> **There is a crucial point in getting rich where thought and personal action must be combined**. There are many people who, consciously or unconsciously, set the creative forces in action (or place their order) by the strength and persistence of their desires, but who remain poor because they do not provide for the reception of the thing they want when it comes; they are not open to receiving it in their life.

By thought, the thing you want is brought to you. By action, you receive it. This is vital information, so critical, that I am going to say it again and I want you to really absorb these words.

By **thought**, the thing you want is **brought** to you.

By **action,** you **receive** it.

In other words, if you have struggled with money all your life, or maybe you've just got by but never really got ahead, then I liken the energy you have in relation to money similar to an invisible force field surrounding you. You can do all the affirmations, visualizations, goal setting and thinking in the world, but when you do attract your desires and they get within 'spitting distance' of you, <u>they can't get through your force field</u>. They simply do not appear in your world because **you do not have an opening for them to enter**.

There is **thought** and there is **action**. You can get out there and do, do, do all day long. But unless your mind is open to receiving wealth, your results will be minimal. You can also go and perch yourself on a mountain top and meditate for wealth, but again, unless you take some action – as they say, "It ain't gonna happen". **You HAVE to marry the two; you MUST combine the metaphysical (thinking and feeling) with the practical (action).**

I recall the story about the man who decided he wanted to win the lottery. He wrote this goal down and chanted it daily. He spent time in quiet meditation, reflecting on the joy of wealth. He repeated his affirmations around winning his millions and visualized himself joyously spending all that cash. The days, which soon turned into weeks, passed and still no big lottery win. Things started to get desperate; he was way behind in his rent and then received notice they were coming to repossess his car.

In a panic he ran out into the back yard, looked up to the heavens, threw his hands up in frustration and yelled. "Lord, you know things have not been going well with my business. I could really use this money. I don't understand, I have been diligently meditating, I've been praying, I've been picturing my big win and saying my affirmations every single.day. I'm doing everything possible but the money isn't here yet. What more could I possibly do?"

A voice booms down from the Heavens and says, "**Meet me halfway...buy a ticket!**"

I love this little story, because it clearly defines the difference between thought and action. <u>The Universe simply cannot deliver if you do not take action</u>. This could be the reason why YOU are not receiving the abundance you have ordered.

As is stated in the teachings of Abraham-Hicks:

"The way the Universe works is quite simple – you have a desire, and it is always answered, every single time."

There are only three points to the fulfillment of your wishes, goals and dreams:

◊ **The creation**, or the asking. That one's easy; it comes naturally – it is what you desire. You really don't have to work on that one at all; it just appears out of nowhere! In the moment you think of what it is you desire, you are asking for that desire.

◊ **The answering to that asking**. That is when the Universe, or God, or Spirit, always gives the answer or 'your order' in the moment you are asking. As I mentioned before, you only have that desire because it's in your warehouse, so the Universe has already provided it. It has answered your call; your desire is on its way.

◊ **YOU must be able to receive**. If there's something that you have been waiting for that is not yet manifesting in your experience, it isn't because of point one (the asking) or point two (the answering or giving), it can only be that you are not in the receiving mode.

So to receive you must take action. You must have an unwavering belief that your desire will appear and you must be grateful (as if it has ALREADY appeared).

 Wildly Wealthy Action Tip

Believe, take action and be grateful.

Write down 3 actions you can take NOW to move you toward your desire (and take those actions TODAY!)

In your Wildly Wealthy FAST Companion Workbook, available from www.WildlyWealthy.com there is an additional Wildly Wealthy Action Exercise.

The Be, Do, Have Secret

'You are only one inch, one step, one idea,
from turning onto the boulevard of beauty in your own life.'
SOMERSET MAUGHAM

The Universe can deliver your order, your dreams, desires and wishes so much faster when you believe it will.

There is a saying, "I'll believe it when I see it". Dr Wayne Dyer a wonderful man many consider to be the 'father of personal development' (and he featured me in a number of his audio programs and books), says that statement is simply not true. The real truth is: **"You'll see it when you believe it"**. In other words, it's only once you actually believe you will have something, that you'll be able to attract it into your life, that it will finally come to pass and you will see it in your physical reality.

One of my clients really wanted a new car – she was sick and tired of driving around in her little bomb. I asked her how she cared for her current car. Did she lovingly wash it and polish it; was she grateful for it and did she treat it with care? "Of course not,' she cried, "it's a bomb"– she thought I was mad. She said there was really no point in looking after her current car, but she promised she'd be extra good when she finally got her new one. I'd given her the formula that never fails – BE, DO, HAVE. This formula is so simple that many ignore the wisdom it offers – as my client did. She believed that once she had the new car then she would put in the effort to clean and polish it, then she would regularly change the oil, then she would make sure no rubbish was dropped inside it and then she would vacuum it out each week. She wanted to Have first, then Be, then Do.

But the winning formula always stays the same. It's Be, Do, Have. First, she would have to BE the person with the new car firmly pictured in her mind, which would cause her to DO the things a person with a beautiful new car would do, and then she would HAVE that car. This formula works for anyone and anything.

Back when I owned my surf wear company around the time of my divorce, I decided I had to work from home as it was so much easier with my young daughter. What I would do, was sew all winter making bikinis and board shorts, t-shirts, wet-shirts etc and then set up a shop for summer at the beginning of the September school holidays. I would sell until Easter in April and then close down. I live at Mooloolaba, a beach side tourist destination on the beautiful Sunshine Coast in Queensland, Australia. It comes alive with people over summer, and then quietens down again for winter. We have one main road that runs along the beach and it is a VERY busy Esplanade. It's packed with shops and cafes and real estate agents. But somehow, every single year for around ten years, there was always an empty store **waiting for me** in the spring.

> *Universal Laws work – whether or not you understand them, whether or not you even know about them – they are working all the time!*

I always knew I would find a place to set up shop. I never doubted it year after year. I just sewed my little heart out all winter, all the time thinking about how much money I would make all summer and picturing what my shop would look like with all the garments I'd made hanging around the store. I totally believed with every ounce of my being that I would once again be on the Esplanade from spring to autumn.

Now back then, I didn't have a clue about the Law of Attraction. I had no idea that what you focus on is what you create. I didn't know anything about Predominant Mental Attitude. **That just goes to show that Universal Laws work – whether or not you understand them, whether or not you even know about them – they are working all the time.**

So just keep your mind on what you do want, just keep focused on the desired outcome. Continue to BE abundant in your mind, strive to DO the things abundant people do, and then you will HAVE the abundance you desire. It will happen, whether or not you understand the how of it. The Universe will bring avalanches of Abundance to you.

 Wildly Wealthy Action Tips

Be – abundant.

Do – whatever it takes.

Have – the life of your dreams.

The More You Give...
The More You Get

'You make a living by what you get,
you make a life by what you give.'
WINSTON CHURCHILL

Congratulations – you are nearly at the end of this book. At this point you should well and truly understand that <u>you can create whatever level of prosperity you desire in your life</u> – purely by continually **focusing on what you do want**, rather than what you don't want. By the time you finish this book, you should be able to proceed through life **with the expectation of continued abundance and unlimited prosperity forever**!

Although the entire book has been advising you on how to improve your lifestyle and have more money, it's time you learnt about a very important law that is a paradox. The Law of the Universe states, <u>the more you give the more you shall receive.</u>

Another secret to becoming wealthy, forever, is to <u>Tithe</u>. The idea of tithing is to give 10% of your income away. **Now before you go freaking out, throwing the book down in horror, deciding you can't go on, manufacturing the excuse that tithing is only for religious zealots, ignoring this chapter altogether or stating you'll wait until you are rich before you tithe,** (yes, I felt all that and more when I first learnt about tithing) understand that of course <u>you do have a choice</u>. Although if you want to be rich, if you want to create the life of your dreams, tithing has to be a part of it!

It's true. Tithing is an <u>important step in guaranteeing your prosperity</u>.

Now, speaking from personal experience, even when I discovered this secret, I simply did nothing about it. The idea of <u>giving away</u>

something that I desperately needed myself made every cell of my being scream in horror! I couldn't bring myself to embrace this strategy. The idea of giving away money scared me. I was struggling financially – **how could I possibly give money away?**

I finally understood about tithing when I read about it in one of Patricia Diane Cota-Robles' books. The purpose behind tithing is that **we have been given the gift of Life** – the ability to think, move, breathe and live in the physical plane. In addition, the Universe has provided everything we need to survive here on Earth: sun for life, water to drink, air to breathe, food to eat, materials to manufacture clothing and shelter. We have chosen to live in a society where we need money to purchase our needs – but **even without money, everything is already provided; everything we need to exist on this planet is already available – for free!** A tithe is simply a way of saying "Thank you" to the Universe. It's more than good manners; it's a Universal Law. The word 'tithe' means 'tenth' and the ancient people felt that 'ten' was the magic number of increase.

> *Money is energy – it expands and returns to you greatly magnified over what you originally sent out.*

Tithing is simply giving money back in appreciation and humble gratitude for just being alive. "But to whom do I give this money?" you may ask. Many people suggest giving to where you are receiving spiritual help and inspiration. Your tithes will then enrich the recipient, allowing that organization, group or individual the freedom to fulfil their highest mission of uplifting mankind. It can be anywhere and to anyone who you feel is enriching your soul spiritually, and if you're not spiritually inclined, then to wherever or whomever you believe is empowering you and allowing you to grow personally. Having said that, I highly recommend giving to any constructive cause or worthwhile organization that makes you feel good — whether that be to charities, needy families, environmental crusaders, animal rights organizations etc. – because it's all about feelings!

Tithing can be a real stumbling block for many people. As I said, my first reaction was, **"I don't even have enough money to pay my weekly bills – how am I supposed to give money away?"**

Natural law is all about give and take. The **attitude and spirit** with which you give this money is **the most important thing about the way you give**. Of course you can give other things; you can give love, time, service, joy, work, and you SHOULD give all these things, but, **like attracts like**, so <u>if you want to increase the money in your life, you must first give money away</u>.

You must also give your tithe away expecting nothing in return from the person or place you give it to. Remember, money is energy like everything else in the Universe and when you send energy (money) out in this way, it **expands and returns to you greatly multiplied or magnified over what you originally sent out.**

Diane states, "If you give as little as 10% of your wealth back to the Universe in gratitude for your gift of life, it will give you <u>such a flow of abundance in your life that you won't be able to handle it all</u>".

Even though you expect nothing in return from the people you give your money to, **you do expect something in return from the Universe and you should claim it.**

For example if you give $100 away, you must consciously say <u>"I now gratefully receive $1000 from the unlimited flow of God's</u> (Spirit's, The Universe's etc.) <u>Abundance for the highest good of all concerned."</u> You should believe **without a shadow of a doubt that the money is winging its way back to you**, and you must feel gratitude as it flows back to you. As already stated "Gratitude unlocks the door to Abundance" and it's an indispensable ingredient toward keeping that flow of money continuing to flow back to you multiplied.

Don't worry about how and from where this money will flow back to you, because then you actually set up blocks for the flow. You only have to believe in your **body,** know in your **mind** and feel in your **soul** that the money is flowing back to you in accordance with Universal Law. Generally, the return does not come back from those you give to. **It comes back from sources you could hardly imagine**.

So it's simple really, <u>if you want to attract more money into your life, you need to give more money away</u>. Do the best you can. As soon as you can start giving money away, do it, <u>even if you start with only a dollar</u>. Don't think you'll start tithing when you are a millionaire. Do you think it's any easier to give away 10% of $1000 than it is to give away 10% of a $1,000,000?

You may think that you don't have anything to give. Yet, if you look more closely, you'll see that even the little you have could be shared with others. Don't wait for a time when you think you'll have lots and then you'll give. By giving and sharing the little you have, you open up the floodgates of the Universe and permit the river of prosperity to flow your way. **You are affirming to the Universe that there IS more than enough, in fact, so much that you can give it away!**

Even God says in Malachi 3:7-12:

> *'Bring ye the whole tithe into the storehouse, that there may be food in my house, and prove me now herewith – if I will not open you the windows of heaven and pour you out a blessing, that there shall not be room enough to receive it.'*

So give away your riches — take a chance on this universal principle. Take a chance on yourself. Universal Laws always work. <u>Sometimes the return from giving happens very quickly</u>. Other times, it takes much longer. But be assured of this: **Give and you will receive and you'll receive lots more than you ever gave.**

When you give, don't do it with a heart of fear, but with a heart full of gratitude. You will be amazed at how it all works out. Open the gates of affluence in your life by giving. As the great Teacher said, "Give and it will be given unto you."

The thing that stops most people from continuous tithing is, <u>they can't track the correlation between the giving and the receiving</u>. You give, and you expect your <u>10% to come back multiplied</u>, but there is no note attached that says – **"This is from the tithe you made 8 June 2004."** It can come in many mysterious and wonderful ways: You get a discount you didn't expect; an old outstanding debt you thought was a lost cause is paid back to you; you get a raise when you weren't expecting one for another year (or two like one of my clients did); you are given an item you really wanted, but couldn't afford; you seal a deal that brings you a huge commission cheque. You finally sell something you have been trying to get rid of for ages or you get stuck behind a huge truck that slows you down and you miss getting a speeding ticket, you meet someone who gives you a contact that allows your business to flourish . <u>You never know where it will come from, but it will come</u>.

You can choose not to tithe, but <u>the Universe will take its 10% anyway</u> (**the opposite** of all the mysterious and wonderful ways it gives to you — as above — may occur!). The thing is, when you don't pay the Universe it will take its portion anyway, (I definitely found this to be true) and **you usually end up paying that 10% plus interest!** So you may as well give where YOU want to.

There are many ways to give; I have given money to organizations whose services have allowed me to grow spiritually. As I am not affiliated with any spiritual organization or church, I feed myself spiritually through the wonderful information others produce. I also give to organizations that uplift and assist others in need.

There are many ways to tithe, but as with everything you learn in this book, <u>it's all about what YOU feel comfortable with,</u> it's all about how you feel. If you really do not, under any circumstances, feel good about tithing to others at this point in your life – **then don't do it**. **I cannot stress this enough**.

If you must, begin the process by tithing to yourself! Just get into the habit of taking that 10% and giving. If it has to be to you at the beginning – I believe that's fine. There will come a time when you feel comfortable giving to others. **You will do more good tithing when it feels right, than doing it now because you think you have to and hating every moment of it.** Just remember you can <u>start with only a dollar</u>. And know that when you do, you will really be opening the floodgates to wealth!

Wildly Wealthy Action Tip

Tithe 10% of your income to whomever and whatever makes you feel good.

Unsure where to give? Visit www.Wildly Wealthy.com for Sandy's suggestions of worthwhile causes.

Give Them Wings

'The more easily you can receive,
the more easily the universe can give to you.'
SANAYA ROMAN AND DUANE PACKER

Within your life, as with everything in nature, there is a flow – a balance which is vital to your growth and expansion. Giving and receiving is part of that flow; you must give in order to receive. However, too many people (particularly women) are so busy giving to everyone else, **they fail to give to the most important person of all – themselves.**

You may think that by giving, giving, giving, you will be blessed and feel fulfilment and joy (which I am sure you do), but if you are only giving and not receiving, you are stopping that never-ending flow. By not allowing yourself to receive you are putting up that barrier for more good to flow to you. Everything is energy, everything is in a constant state of movement, and everything is flowing. You must be open to receive everything – more love, more money, more friendship, more compliments, more health, more time, more happiness, more laughter, and more joy; **more of everything.** The more you receive, the more you can give! Start practising receiving MORE today!

The other aspect of giving all the time is that you can become someone else's support – they rely on you, instead of finding their own feet and taking total responsibility for themselves. They expect (maybe only at a subconscious level) that you will rescue them. **You are actually hindering their growth** by giving (your time, energy, money) all the time.

A man once found a cocoon. After a time a small opening appeared and he sat and watched the butterfly for several hours as it struggled to force its body through that little hole. Then it seemed to stop making any progress. It appeared as if it had gotten as far as it could, and it could go no further. So the man decided to help the butterfly. He took a pair of scissors and snipped away the remaining part of the cocoon. The butterfly then emerged easily. But it had a swollen body and small shrivelled wings. The man continued to watch because at any moment he expected the wings would enlarge and expand to support the body, which would contract in time. Neither happened! In fact, the butterfly spent the rest of its short life crawling around with a swollen body and shrivelled wings. It never was able to fly.

What the man, in his kindness and haste, did not understand was the restricting cocoon and the struggle required for the butterfly to get through the tiny opening were God's way of forcing fluid from the body of the butterfly into its wings so that it would be ready for flight once it achieved its freedom from the cocoon. **Sometimes struggle is exactly what we need in our lives**. If God allowed us to go through our lives without any obstacles, it would cripple us. We would not be as strong as we could have been. We could never fly!

This is a lesson that can be challenging to put into practice when you are finally in the position of being able to help others financially. When you have more, you naturally want to give more. You don't want others, particularly those close to you, to have to go through what you did, you want to ease their burden.

So teach them what you have learned; show them how you did it. Give them the knowledge and assist them to create for themselves. Don't weaken them by making it easy for them – if they're ready to listen, share the principles in this book. "Give a man a fish, you feed him for a day, teach a man to fish and you feed him for a life-time". Do you want to help those you love for a day and then watch them struggle for the rest of their lives, or **be the one that shows them how to use their wings and soar**?

I actually learnt this the hard way, through borrowing from others. It wasn't until I had no-one to turn to, until I could no longer borrow any more money from anyone, until my back was against the wall and I thought it was all over, that I took total responsibility, not only for where I was, but for making sure I changed my circumstances. I took charge of my financial situation, I applied all I had learnt (I used to be extremely good at learning, learning, learning – but not applying!) and things actually turned around totally for me.

Watching people struggle can be extremely challenging if you have been in that same position yourself; you don't want others to have to go through it, **you just want to help**; you want to give and you want to ease their pain. My advice is, if at all possible — **don't give them a handout. You are cutting their cocoon**. Instead, give them a hand up — <u>give them wings so they can fly</u>. Give them knowledge, so they too can transform their world.

'Formal education will make you a living;
self-education will make you a fortune.'
JIM ROHN

 Wildly Wealthy Action Tip

Enjoy receiving, this will open the flow.

Teach others to fly – give them a hand up rather than a hand out.

Do You Feel Rich?

'I don't think you have to chase success,
but I do think you need to slow down long enough
for it to catch you.'

RICHARD CARLSON

You may be putting into practice a lot of the tips and secrets in this book, but nothing is showing up, something is missing. As taught by Abraham-Hicks — there is a spiritual law that says **you cannot attract from the opposite of what you desire**. In other words, you cannot attract thin, when you feel fat. You cannot attract love, when you feel unloved. You cannot attract riches, when you feel poor. I can hear you already… "How ridiculous", "I'm broke, and I feel broke, so that means I will be broke forever? What's the point of all this?"

The point is, you have to change the way you feel inside, to change what happens on the outside – "<u>As within, so without</u>".

You **cannot practise the ideas in this book on a superficial level and expect to see mountains of money come your way**. You have to 'feel it in your bones' to attract it into the physical world. It doesn't mean you have to feel exactly like a millionaire

> *You cannot practise the ideas in this book on a superficial level and expect to see mountains of money come your way.*

feels to attract more wealth; you just have to embrace the feeling of richness, whatever that is for you. What do YOU think wealthy people do? **What for YOU constitutes living a life of richness and abundance?**

It doesn't have to be earth-shattering, mind-blowing, fire-hose riches. <u>You're just starting the trickle, not asking for the entire flood</u>. Doing something that makes you feel rich is going to be something entirely different for everyone. For me, it was the luxury of having my house cleaned. I may have mentioned – I do NOT like cleaning and I am NO housewife! Even though I was struggling financially, I knew that people who were rich must have someone else clean their house. (Surely, I reasoned, they wouldn't do it themselves if someone was willing to do it for them!)

Paying someone to clean my house was really blowing the budget, but I knew, if I could walk into my home and have it spotless, and I wasn't the one to make it that way, then I would feel incredibly wealthy! So I paid someone to come for an hour and a half once a month to clean my home and it cost me around $22. And I was right. Seeing the floor sparkling clean, the stove shining and the bathrooms gleaming, and knowing I had nothing to do with it, **made me feel incredibly rich!** I have a cleaner in every week now, and <u>still feel that wonderful feeling every time it's done!</u>

> *Once wealth and riches become part of who you are internally, they will show up in your life!*

Create /Experience/Enjoy Feeling Rich...

◊ Have a massage

◊ Buy fresh flowers every week

◊ Go to a day spa

◊ Hire a Porsche (or your favourite car) for the day

◊ Go to a restaurant and don't even look at the prices

◊ Have someone come in and clean your house

◊ Take your best friends out to lunch

◊ Buy a special food you usually go without

◊ Go to the theatre

◇ Visit the opera

◇ Have a manicure and pedicure

And the great thing is, you don't actually have to spend money to feel rich! I often like to drop my children off at school, then go down to the ocean for a swim. Being at the beach, jumping through the waves, feeling the sun on my skin when I know everyone else is stuck inside working, really makes me feel Wildly Wealthy!

Feel Rich for free:

◇ Pick a bunch of flowers

◇ Take a picnic to the beach at sunset

◇ Go for a drive in an expensive estate and imagine which house you now own

◇ Go window shopping where 'rich people shop' feeling as if you have a million dollars in your bank account. Choose what you'll buy later when the money really appears!

◇ Visit an Art Gallery

◇ Go to a wine tasting

◇ Join the Millionaire Money Game at www.MillionaireMoneyGame.com

◇ Listen to Mozart (it's been proven to make you feel rich!)

◇ Luxuriate in a bubble bath by candlelight

◇ Walk through display homes, choosing the design and décor for your own dream house.

◇ Browse on-line or through magazines and catalogues, to find pictures for your Vision Board!

Whether it's free or something you have to buy – try and do at least one thing on a daily or weekly basis that makes you **FEEL rich**. Make sure you consistently do something that you just **KNOW rich people do**. A quick note – do NOT go into debt to practise this one; make sure you spend only what you have in cash and what is easily affordable.

The more you practise feeling rich, the faster it becomes a part of you. **Once wealth and riches become part of who you are internally**, <u>they will show up in your life</u>! So start practising today!

 Wildly Wealthy Action Tip

Make a list of at least 20 things that make YOU feel rich.

Make sure you do AT LEAST one of these each week!

When It All Goes Wrong... Get Excited!

'Mama told me there'd be days like this.'
VAN MORRISON

Have you ever experienced everything going along 'swimmingly', when out of the blue the 'mud hits the fan'? "Why is this so?" you may ask. Why do these things happen when you've really been **thinking wonderful thoughts, focusing on creating absolute masses of money in your life, visualizing, affirming, sending love out in all directions and generally doing the right thing**? Two things you must remember. You are a creator; your thoughts are things. You send them out into the world and then attract back to you those that are most predominant. Before you came across this book, you may have been focusing on the lack in your life, day after day, for years. You may have some 'backorders for lack' to clear before you really embrace the avalanches of Abundance that you have now ordered.

You are not yet an instant creator; you have a lag time between what you think, and when it arrives. Therefore, if you are experiencing some potholes in your road to riches, just keep focused on the future, your ideal future, and you will get there. Don't 'keep an eye on those potholes' or you may have an even bigger crash!

The other thing to remember is, even though you may be really committed to everything you have learnt through the pages of this book, things **may still seem to go awry**. You may be putting all the steps together and little by little, you are attracting more into your life when suddenly – BAM – it all appears to go wrong. You seem to be going backwards and things start going downhill fast. Don't panic.

You are part of nature, you are made up of flesh and blood and cells and atoms. You are who you are not just on a surface level, but also on a cellular level. When you are putting all these processes into place, there may come a time when you feel very uncomfortable. The reason for this is you're 'giving birth' to a new creation. **You have to change who you are on a cellular level** to become a new and improved you, so you can accept new and improved events, situations and people into your life.

This can be very confronting for most people and often it's in this moment of moving out of your comfort zone that you actually surrender to the uncomfortable feelings and give up. Let me give you an example: You decide you are better than your current job, and so you apply for that fantastic opportunity at that great new company. You send in your resume, go for the interview and it all goes well and you think you have a good chance of getting the job. You get a phone call to say you have been short-listed – can you come in on Thursday for a final interview?

Then suddenly, things start to go wrong. You begin to wonder if this new job is right for you, or whether you are right for it. You start to feel sick in the pit of your stomach. At the last minute your boss gives you a project that has to be finished by Thursday midday. You go home and feel as if you are getting a slight fever; maybe you're getting a cold. Thursday comes and you are too sick to get out of bed, let alone finish your project and get to the interview. You even convince yourself that these 'signs' are proof that you should stay where you are. But what actually happened? I'll tell you what happened – you were getting incredibly close to manifesting your desire – that's it!

> *The Universe always wants bigger and better for you than you do for yourself.*

When something moves from the metaphysical or the 'formless' into the physical plane, it's almost as if it has to cross some invisible barrier. When it hits that barrier, **things start to change, things begin to transform, and things can get ugly**. It only means that it is all falling into place the way it should. The thing is, you can't see the big picture – you don't know what the Universe's grand plan is. But remember, the Universe always wants bigger and better for you than you do for yourself. But you focus on the here and now, you see things as they are and fall to pieces wondering, "Why me?"

I remember back to one of my many business ventures. I came across these really great little slippers that used magnet therapy and reflexology. They were tiny (only came to under the arch of your foot and your heel hung over the end) but they actually helped you to lose weight. The concept behind them was that the realignment of the spine helped to rid you of back, shoulder and neck pain, and balance you from the inside out, thereby increasing your metabolism, which in turn burned fat and the weight would drop off easily. They definitely worked – I used them, my back pain disappeared and I lost about 5kg without changing my eating or exercising habits! So my idea was to bring them in from China, set up a website and sell them. I used the power of my mind (and plenty of phone calls) to get a TV station to do a story on them.

I was so pumped up – I was excited beyond belief – this was it. Here I was, about to have my new venture on TV and then import a whole container load of these slippers. The people at the TV station told me that stories on either making money or losing weight generated the most interest. **I should expect hundreds if not thousands of enquiries**. As I said, I was excited. This, I had decided, was going to pull me out of the hole; this was going to make me rich beyond my wildest dreams. I was going to sell SlimSlippers all around Australia, pay off all my debts and live the life of my dreams! **It was all about to happen for me and I was ready!**

The story was set to go to air on Thursday, but there were extra stories they had to run, so it was changed to Friday, but again, no time. Then it was definitely scheduled for Monday. I was SO excited. All weekend I was jumping out of my skin, Monday my life was going to change forever… then, over the weekend, tragedy occurred in Bali – the bombing of innocent lives. Yes, my story went to air Monday night, with a story about the Bali bombing right before it, and a special about the Bali bombings right after it. Who in their right mind would be focusing on silly little SlimSlippers with all that tragedy going on? Well, at least twelve people I guess, as that's how many orders I received after the show.

Was the queen of personal development upset in any way? You bet I was; **I was shattered, I was despondent, I was depressed, I was down lower than low**. I could not believe what had happened. "Why me? What had I done to deserve this? Why did things always go wrong for me? What is the matter with me?" Things could not have looked any worse for me at that point than they did. I got upset and I moaned and I groaned and I sobbed and I screamed and generally lost the plot (for a few hours only). I was so far down the financial gurgler that I didn't see any way to get back up. That's when I went out and got my part-time job at the clothing shop, and that's when, just a few weeks later, I started my direct sales business that led me to where I am today.

You see **the Universe knows what's going on**. I had my sights set on a SlimSlippers empire – and if my plan had all worked out, I would be selling those little slippers, posting parcels all over Australia, getting returns, dealing with irate customers because they got the wrong size etc. etc. And instead, here I am living my life's purpose. I'm living my dream, teaching people around the world how to create a life filled with Prosperity, showing them that **it is possible, and anyone can do it, including YOU**!

Yet, if my SlimSlippers business had gone as planned, do you think I would have bothered speaking to my Accountant about the direct sales business, which ultimately led me to where I am today – **NOT ON YOUR LIFE**. I wouldn't have had the time; I would have had the perfect excuse NOT to talk with my Accountant! I would have continued doing small prosperity classes every few months, fitting that in around posting out those tiny little slippers!

The Universe HAD to mess it up so I didn't miss the opportunity that ultimately lead me to my destiny.

The Universe has listened to your request and heard your order. It knows what is best for you in the long run; it has its own 'grand plan'. It has to re-arrange your life so you can receive those things you ordered – but it could get a little messy (just like cleaning out that garage!)

I have discovered a way to get the most out of my worst moments… **Get Excited!** That's right; get excited. You must fully understand the following statement: <u>the Universe loves you, adores you, wants nothing but good for you</u>, and sometimes it looks like it's getting worse, because it's changing course to something so much better than you could ever dream of. **When things go wrong, <u>get excited</u>, do a happy dance and try to imagine what miraculous thing is going to occur in your life**. I have found a fairly equal correlation between how bad something seems and how good it ultimately turns out. That's not to say you must always have a downer in your life before anything good happens. It's just my own experience has often been, the worse a situation has looked, the more fantastic the outcome in the long run.

That's the time to get out your list of desires, spend some time visualizing your dreams, listen to an inspiring audio-program or dance to your favourite music CD; **do whatever you can to pull your energy back up because what you want is on the way!**

Get excited about **<u>what is going to happen</u>**, not what is **currently happening!** Don't think about how bad things are; don't tell your parents how tragic it is; don't phone your friends to share the horrible news – because then you are **focusing more on the bad**, and you are actually pushing the good the Universe is trying to bring you, away. <u>You are refusing the gift from God, and placing an order for more bad.</u>

It's in those uncomfortable moments that you should close your eyes and see the truck backing up to your warehouse. Fill your body with excitement – **and know that something wonderful is making its way from the formless, unseen, metaphysical plane, into this physical plane.** Just remind yourself that you have to have darkness for the stars to shine, and there has to be a storm for you to see the rainbow.

From now on, if things go wrong, fill your body with anticipation knowing that the Universe has something special in store for you! When the going gets rough for you, it is merely a confirmation that you are set to grow even richer, have even more wealth and live an increasingly abundant life. **So get excited!**

Wildly Wealthy Action Tip

Get excited if things seem to take a turn for the worse; anticipate something wonderful appearing in your life!

The Most Powerful
Force in the Universe

'It's a marvellous night for a moondance,
with the stars up above in the sky.'
VAN MORRISON

In order to be Rich, if you are not rich now, you are going to be in a constant state of tension, because you are stretching and moving out of your comfort zone — the only way to relax in that state of tension is to **feel it often enough that you get used to it;** in other words, practise the strategies in this book daily.

If you were unfit and decided to run a marathon, but only trained really hard once a week, and the rest of the time sat around and ate junk food — you would always be sore, always in pain, and you'd never run that marathon. It's the same with being rich. If you focus on being rich and think about it once a week, and the rest of the time focus on your debts and money problems, you will always be in tension and you will never be rich. You must 'train' daily; think about wealth, picture wealth, feel wealth, dream of all you will do with your wealth. **Do it daily. And you will be rich!**

> *Think about wealth, picture wealth, feel wealth, dream of all you will do with your wealth. Do it daily. And you will be rich.*

If you persist, then your world will change. As with anything new, it can sometimes seem like too much effort (and we all want results yesterday!). You will have to remember to make time for and practise your strategies and exercises. It may even seem like a chore – <u>but don't think of it that way!!</u> The second you have that feeling, you lose energy, you lower your vibration, you attract from a place of lack.

'We all know that a rocket burns most of its fuel
during the first few moments of flight as it overcomes inertia
and the gravitational pull of the earth.
That's what it's like for us as we launch
our dreams into physical reality.'

MARIA NEMETH, PH.D.

Day by day, as you repeat the various strategies in this book, you will enjoy them more and more, you will embrace them, they will become part of who you are and then you will do them automatically. You will begin to see evidence that you have tapped into that great river of Abundance. Then life becomes a joy. You are in the flow and you will be a money magnet!

The following affirmation is the most powerful and fun of all the strategies I teach (in my humble opinion). This is wonderful to do with a group of people. With the synergy that is created, the power that is unleashed, and the magnetizing that occurs – look out Universe!

Fill your body with as much emotion and energy as you can. Don't just say the words; feel them. Feel the wealth, feel the energy, feel that love flowing to you in the form of money; feel it coming directly from the Universe. <u>Those feelings are what will make your words magnetic and attract your desire back to you.</u> And make sure you include your physical body as well; use your arms!

As you say "I call…" stretch your arms out wide and high, palms to the heavens, fingers outstretched as if you are reaching for something (which you are!). As you call the Prosperity etc. to you — when you say, "Come to me now" — actually physically grab onto it with your hands (I should say metaphysically grab it, because you can't yet see it on the physical plane, but it IS there!) and pull it in toward your solar plexus — that area above your navel. The solar plexus is recognised as the power centre of the body; it's where you assimilate feelings such as the intense emotions of laughter and joy. You want more money in your life? <u>Then make sure you activate this area as you say this affirmation</u>. Then at the very end, when you affirm, "**And I love it**", fling your arms high and wide with outstretched hands and create a funnel, a channel for the Universe to pour an ever increasing flow of abundance starting at your fingertips, down to your heart and through your entire being so you are overflowing with Prosperity!

Say this affirmation slowly; say it fast; whisper it softly or shout it out to the Universe – but **fill it with emotion and feeling** and it will do amazing things for you!

If you would like to utilise the power of a Mastermind, you can listen to a recording of The Abundance Affirmation and say it with me by going to <u>www.WildlyWealthy.com</u>. You will also find a copy of this affirmation there to print off and keep!

Remember to <u>fill your words, your body, your heart and your soul with emotion</u>…

Abundance Affirmation

I am unlimited

I now consciously and subconsciously flood every atom of my body, mind and spirit with Prosperity Consciousness.

I bless everyone in the Universe to have Abundance and Prosperity.

I give myself permission to deserve and expect
Abundance and Prosperity.

I call Abundance and Prosperity from the four corners of the earth and throughout the Universe.

Prosperity in the north, south, east and west – come to me now!

Abundance in the north, south, east and west – come to me now!

Money in the north, south, east and west – come to me now!

Riches in the north, south, east and west – come to me now!

Wealth in the north, south, east and west – come to me now!

And so it is – **and I love it!**

This affirmation has so much power; it unleashes a force that the Universe simply cannot ignore! You will feel energized, alive and magnetic to prosperity. You will be able to feel that <u>money is winging its way to you immediately!</u> Don't be shy with this affirmation – make sure the Universe hears you **loud and clear**!

I remember sitting in my bedroom chanting these words, and in the distance, I could hear a little voice from my son's bedroom as he was playing with his Action Man (he was nine at the time) chanting those same words. I must have said it so often that he knew the words by heart!

There are some particularly great times and places that I love to use this affirmation. I live on a part of Australia's beautiful coastline that has a huge headland jutting out of the ocean. It's a magical place where the powerful ocean rolls in day after day and standing there looking at the horizon you feel 'at one' with the Universe. I love to go there when there is a full moon. As the huge orange ball rises out of the ocean, I begin my affirmation. I remember having my son there once, and he told me he was 'standing on guard' to make sure no-one was coming. He didn't mind thinking I was crazy, but he didn't want anyone else to!

Other powerful times are under the stars at night, lying on a beach, being deep in a forest or sitting on a mountain. You know, it really doesn't matter where you use the Abundance Affirmation, because it is strong, powerful and sends out a very clear order to the Universe for more money NOW! <u>It ignites something deep within your soul</u> **that causes you to immediately become more magnetic to prosperity, wealth, abundance and riches**!

 Wildly Wealthy Action Tip

Say the Abundance Affirmation daily and feel your spirit soar.

The More You Want, The Less You Get

'Always… that which you most need is already at hand.
It is simply your incessant searching and belief in its absence,
that keeps it from view.'

MIKE DOOLEY

It's funny how, quite often, the more you chase after something – for instance, wealth – the more it runs away. The more desperately you need money, the more it eludes you. The more every cell of your being cries out to fill your bank account, the bigger the financial hole becomes. Why is this so? Simple really – it's all to do with detachment.

Detachment is the process of releasing what you want to the Universe.

Detachment is the understanding that you know what you want, and you believe the Universe will bring you what is best for your highest good.

Your steps to attracting should be:

◊ Become clear on what it is you desire

◊ Write down your desire

◊ Visualize your desire as already in your life

◊ Feel your desire deep inside and know it's already yours

◊ Feel grateful it's yours

◊ Confirm your order by taking action

◊ **Then let it go. You must detach.**

It's not that you no longer care about what you've asked for – because you certainly still do. It's not that you don't want it – because you want it more than ever. It's just that you are no longer attached to the outcome. You stop worrying about when it's coming, how it's coming and if it's coming. If it comes it comes; if it doesn't, then that's OK too. Speaking from experience, this can be a **very challenging thing to do, particularly when you are broke and you want more money!**

You see, **when you are so strongly attached to the outcome**, to getting something – in this case more money – **you are needy;** and when you are needy, **your energy is saying you don't have it**, and when your energy is saying you don't have it, that is the order you send to the Universe. So the Universe fills your 'don't have it' order and you get more of not having it.

If your **energy is very strongly focused on you not having received your desire yet, your energy is coming from noticing that it's not there**. And noticing it's not there, will keep it not there. That energy will keep you separated from your desire forever more. Worrying about how it will come, when it will come and if it will come, will keep it

> *In that moment, behind the scenes, your life turns around; all sorts of things conspire to finally bring you your heart's desire.*

away! But once you detach, once you let go of the outcome and feel wonderful for where your life is right here and now, you open a doorway for your desire to appear!

How often have you heard of a couple wanting a child so badly, they count days, take temperatures, practise at every available opportunity, and do everything they can – but still, no baby. They may even go so far as to try IVF, and still nothing happens. They finally resign themselves to a life without a child – they let go of the idea – and bingo, thank you very much – suddenly someone's pregnant! A miracle? Absolutely… but they created that miracle by letting go, by suddenly being OK with what they had. And by accepting where they were, the door opened and what they desired was able to enter.

Maybe you have heard the following:

"The tide has to get to its lowest ebb before it can turn"
or

"You have to hit rock bottom before you can climb back up"

Most people assume that these sayings mean things have to get really rotten before they can get any better. And yes, this is quite often the case, but **only because most people wait until things are so bad before they finally detach.**

If you desire something so much you are obsessing over it, you will feel very separated from your desire. You will be consumed with your desire, or more accurately the lack of your desire! You look to see if it's appeared in your life, you try and work out when it's coming, you try and plan how and when the Universe will deliver (which you will NEVER be able to figure out!), but it still doesn't come. You start to feel maybe it will never happen.

You think your order has been forgotten and you get busy doing other things and BINGO – **it suddenly appears when you least expect it**. Why? Usually because you've given up. You've finally detached. You've stopped plotting and planning and scheming how the Universe will give you what you want. You've thought, quite wrongly, that the Universe is not on your side and stopped caring about it altogether. You've done what you should have done at the beginning – you've detached.

Now don't get me wrong, it's not that the Universe wants you to 'give up on your desires' before it will deliver. It's just that in that moment, when you decide **it doesn't matter any more** – if what you want comes, wonderful, but if it doesn't, you'll survive, that you allow the Universe to do its job. It's when you stop obsessing about what it is you want and get busy doing other things that you then release the tight 'force field' type energy you are holding around your desire and it can come to you.

It's when you finally accept and feel grateful for your life as it is, when you no longer feel emotionally obsessed with your desire, that you finally detach. And in that moment, behind the scenes, your life turns around; **all sorts of things conspire to finally bring you your heart's desire.** Mind you, life can be so much easier if you detach, if you let go, BEFORE you hit rock bottom!

The idea is to **stay at one with your desire**, see it, feel it in your bones and let it fill your body, mind and spirit. Let it feel so alive within you that the feeling, seeing and believing is enough for you – you feel as if you already have it, then detach. The added bonus is, by detaching you are allowing the Universe to deliver. So start detaching from the outcome and you too will experience riches beyond your wildest dreams!

 Wildly Wealthy Action Tip

Stay at one with your desire (see it, feel it, love it!) and detach from the outcome.

Ride On the Wings
of Prosperity

'You are a magnificent, powerful person,
and you can learn to work with your energy to tap into the
unlimited abundance of the universe.
Creating money can be effortless, the natural outcome
of the way you live, think, and act.
You can draw anything you want to you; you can realize
your fondest dreams.'

ORIN AND DABEN

Have you ever felt 'in the flow'? Ever felt like anything is possible? Has there been a time when everything was going so well, things just fell into place? Have you ever noticed that when someone has one success, it's often the beginning of a string of successes? They just seem to 'get lucky'. "How do they do it?" you may ask. "What's their secret?" Well, **you're about to learn how to take a quantum leap toward prosperity!**

I'm sure you know how difficult it is if your car has broken down and you have to get out and push it off the road. Just getting it rolling takes the most muscle; it takes enormous effort and almost seems impossible, but once you get started, it takes on a life of its own – it's easy to keep it going. In fact, once you get started you have to watch that it doesn't take off and leave you behind.

> *You're about to learn how to take a quantum leap toward prosperity!*

It's the same with you and money! Why not use that same principle to attract more prosperity into your life? When something happens, maybe you find five cents on the footpath, maybe you receive a 10% discount at your favourite store, maybe you go to the mail box and find a cheque for $5.00 which is a refund for an overpayment – it doesn't matter how much, or where the prosperity comes from, **it is evidence that you are already in the flow!** You are attracting money; **it's proof you're already in that prosperous vibration. Make the most of it!**

It's in these moments that **you should call more prosperity to you**. It's as if the money is already showing up - even in small amounts — so you should say your Affirmations and feel the Abundance flowing to you. When you see the evidence of more abundance, you should take the time to passionately feel your desire, your ultimate vision, deep within your heart. It's during the already evident flow of prosperity that you could take a moment and do some Abundance Breaths. It is in this prosperous vibration that you could visualize yourself as having already received your desires. It is now that you could kiss your money and let it know just how much you love it!

> *When you see the evidence of more abundance, you should take the time to passionately feel your desire, your ultimate vision, deep within your heart.*

When you're in the flow — make the most of it. It's in those moments that your channel, **your direct link to the Universe is fully open,** fully connected and that powerful source is receiving your message loud and clear. So send those orders through for a super fast delivery service!

The other time you can easily tap into the abundance flow is **when you are really happy.** That's right, when you are having fun, when you are laughing, when you are filled with joy, your vibration is already way 'up there'. You are emotionally and spiritually 'light' – you usually even feel physically lighter! It's easier to attract more of what you want when you're already on that light, high, prosperous vibration. Laughter is one of the most expansive levels of energy and **causes your desires to become magnetically energized and attracted into your life very quickly!**

I remember when I was just starting my very first direct sales business. I was far too scared to talk to anyone I knew, so I would put ads in the local paper and people who were interested in my product could phone me. The thing was, I would sit there all day Saturday, as close to the phone as possible and check my voice mail every fifteen minutes, hoping I would have another message. Usually from one ad I would get around 10 calls or less, if I had 15 or more I was feeling **really lucky!** Saturday and usually Sunday was devoted to checking my ad responses. I didn't call them until Monday, but I just **had to be there.**

It was around this time a friend invited me to go away for the weekend. He was talking on personal development to a group of sales people up in the beautiful Bunya Mountains and suggested I come and listen and we could stay in one of the little chalets. He said we could take bush walks and light a huge roaring fire in the open fireplace – it sounded like fun. "But", I thought, "I have two ads going in the paper, I can't possibly go away — I have to check my messages!" He was intelligent, good looking and a really fun guy, so it didn't take too much convincing to get me to leave my phone for the weekend. And we **really did have the most wonderful time,** laughing, walking in the huge forests, laughing again, cosying up in front of a crackling fire, laughing, talking about the power of the mind and how to create, and laughing some more!

Before I knew it the weekend was over and we were on our way home. There was a 'no phone' rule while we were away, so on the drive home I checked my voice-mail. "You have 84 messages" it said, I couldn't believe my ears; I was expecting the usual ten or so. Eighty-four – how did this happen, I wasn't there, willing the messages to come to me all day long, how did I get so many? All in all, I received just over 100 enquiries from the two ads – that's around ten times more than usual. And the reason was – I was **detached from the outcome, and I was having fun.** It's an amazing combination!

When you're laughing with your children, when you're having fun with your friends, when you're really full of love, happiness and joy, that's when anything is possible. It's a great idea to get clear on what you want, focus on your desire, place your order, and **then go and have fun** – you are putting in your order and then detaching, which allows it to wing it's way to you so much faster. Having fun and prosperity go hand in hand – so have some fun today!

 Wildly Wealthy Action Tips

Use laughter and fun to become more magnetic to money.

Focus on Prosperity and your desires when you are already attracting more (big or small) and you will ride on the Wings of Prosperity.

Show Me The Money!

'I will persist until I succeed.
The prizes of life are at the end of each journey,
not near the beginning...
Failure I may still encounter at the thousandth step,
yet success hides behind the next bend in the road.
Never will I know how close it lies unless I turn the corner.'
OG MANDINO

Congratulations. You made it! You have covered an enormous amount of information through this book. More importantly, if you have applied all the Wildly Wealthy Action Tips you should now be experiencing dramatic changes in your financial life. But what if you have read all the wonderful ideas, tips, strategies, exercises and secrets and you're still not getting the results you desire. What if nothing has shown up?

Well, to be honest, if you have been **applying the Wildly Wealthy Action Tips**, it would be impossible for nothing to have happened. We are talking about Universal Law here; <u>it HAS to happen! If you are applying it consistently, there can be no other outcome</u>!

What may happen is, you read the book and think it has been wonderful to learn all these secrets, in fact you may have already known some of them. But you must keep in mind: learning and knowing is one thing, doing is another. Learning moves that knowledge into your head, <u>doing or action moves it into your heart so it becomes a part of who you are</u>. **You must take action and apply these steps**.

I am often asked if my life is a continual flood of riches and prosperity. My answer is, "Yes, I have definitely discovered the secrets to limitless Abundance. Although, being human, there are also days and sometimes weeks when I feel my source is drying up!" It's in those moments I feel I have lost my 'magic wand' and I wonder if my Midas touch is tarnished. Thankfully these moments are few and far between, but when it does happen, it forces me to take a long look at where I am in my life and what I am doing on a daily basis. If you are experiencing a 'dry spell' – you must do the same.

Often it's because you have **become too busy living life day to day**, and not taking the time to do what is important. It could be you haven't been saying your affirmations or feeling rich. Maybe you have accumulated too much clutter and your energy has become scattered. Often it is because you are not nurturing your body, mind and spirit and it reflects in what is showing up in your life. **It's not enough to know or even write about abundance, you must BE abundance… you must LIVE abundance**.

> *It's not enough to know or even write about abundance; you must BE abundance… you must LIVE abundance.*

The exciting thing is, it doesn't matter if you've never been in the flow, or you've just stepped out of it for a little while — **it's easy to get back in there**! You just have to take stock of where you are now, what you are consistently doing, and continually make changes for the better. I've devised the following checklist for you to revisit at any time to keep yourself on track, so you can see, step-by-step, if you are **living Abundance**!

Go through this checklist to see if there is anything you have missed and should focus on so you can become **Wildly Wealthy even faster!** Only check it if you can definitely say YES. Remember, you don't have to do every single thing daily (although the more the merrier), as long as you **do something every single day**.

💰 Have you made a **Prosperity Binder** to keep all your information, thoughts and ideas around Abundance and Prosperity together and easy to find? Take time to look at it daily. Keep your focus on wealth.

💰 Have you **written down your Intentions** and what you would like to see happen in your life over the next 2-6 months? **Dream big and expect to receive it**.

💰 Are you doing your **Abundance Breaths daily**, and are you really <u>feeling that Abundance flowing</u> through your body? Can you see and feel the Prosperity flooding every cell of your being?

💰 Have you **gone on a media diet**, or even a fast? Are you using those spare hours **to focus on your prosperity and wealth?**

💰 Are you writing in your **Grateful Journal** every day? Are you filling your body with gratitude throughout the day?

💰 Are you remembering to **feel grateful for everything that you already have** in your life? The more you are grateful, the more you will attract things into your life to be grateful for.

💰 Are you **envisioning your desires as already having manifested and feeling grateful for them**? Gratitude is a powerful emotion that will bring you what you desire rapidly if you can feel thankful as if you already have them.

💰 Are you **saving 10%** of everything you make? This is an indispensable step to your financial freedom. Open a special account and start immediately!

💰 Do you **save all your coins** and get excited each time you bank them?

💰 Have you **cleared out your clutter** to make way for the new? You will feel your energy flowing faster when your life is free of clutter. The Universe is just waiting for you <u>to make space to bring in the new.</u>

💰 Have you **sold off your no longer needed items**, or donated them to charity?

💰 Have you put any **money from items sold into your special savings account or towards paying off your debts?**

💰 Is your **predominant mental attitude** on Wealth, Prosperity and Abundance? Are your **words aligning with your desires**? You can't be focused on Abundance and then cancel it with your words. Watch your self-talk and the conversations you have with others. You must be consistently speaking words that are in alignment with your greatest desires.

- Are you **saying your affirmations consistently with strong feelings**? Remember, feelings create, so flood the words with your emotions to make them magnetic.

- Are you **having fun paying your bills**? Do you spend your money with feelings of gratitude and love? Remember, you have to love money flowing out as well as loving the flow in.

- Do you **love saving money on items daily**? Are you doing this from a place of enthusiasm and expansion or from a place of lack and limitation? Your enthusiasm for putting that saved money **into your special savings account or to pay off debts** is what allows you to continue to attract more money to you.

- Do you **kiss your money and feel love for your money** and feel love flowing back from your money? Money, like everything in this Universe, is energy and will be attracted to like energy. Show your money how much you love it and it will want to spend more time with you!

- Have you visited www.WildlyWealthyWomen.com to get **additional free prosperity resources**?

- Have you **made a Vision Board with pictures that make your heart sing?** Looking at visual images is the key to attracting and will keep your desires alive and energised.

- Do you have some of **your affirmations on your wall where you can see them constantly**? Give them even more energy by saying them before you go to sleep each night.

- Have **you detached from your desires**? Can you think about Prosperity and Abundance without feeling the lack of it in your life right now? **Feel at one with your desires right now;** feel the love in your heart for already having received riches **and detach emotionally from the outcome.**

- **Are you nurturing yourself?** The more you look after your body, mind and spirit, the higher your vibration will be and the **faster you will attract** your desires into your life.

- 💰 **Are you feeling love** – for yourself, for others, for your life, for the money you have, for the money you know is coming? Love is a powerful magnet. Love binds the Universe.

- 💰 Do you make the choice to **go without rather than go into debt**? Have you stopped using your credit card, or only use it responsibly?

- 💰 Have you **made the commitment not to take on any more bad debt** of any kind – ever?

- 💰 Have you **listed your debts** and made a plan to pay them off? **Do you celebrate** as even the smallest debt is finalised?

- 💰 Do you **use the Alpha state to create**? This is a powerful time to think and feel your desires into creation. As you go to sleep and as you wake up, picture your desires — whether that is a certain amount of money, a dream house, new car, trip overseas or even a new love — as already in your life. Feel how good it feels to have achieved your desire — let it flood your body.

- 💰 You understand the power of a Mastermind, and the power of your words, do you **speak only of what you do want to create** with your friends?

- 💰 Are you **opening your Treasure Chest** and feeling at one with your desires as you drift off to sleep?

- 💰 Do you **create a vision of your desires in your mind** in great detail? Do you see yourself in that vision? Do you feel yourself in that vision? Do you feel at one with that vision?

- 💰 Do you **track your money**? If so, you should be now making better spending choices. This **frees up your energy on a metaphysical level,** and will keep your logical mind happy and occupied, allowing more prosperity to flow into your life.

- 💰 Have you **written a Desire Statement**? Did you include all the things you wanted to see in your life? You can write a Desire Statement for your health, for your relationships, for...**anything you desire**.

- 💰 Have you **made the decision to persist** until you are Wildly Wealthy? Have you put it in writing and let the Universe know you are committed to doing whatever it takes to create the life of your dreams?

Are you **creating extra income** through a job or business? Are you loving the money that comes to you? Are you doing what you love? If your job or business is long term, doing what you love will help you to create feelings of enthusiasm and fulfilment. These emotions enable you to **raise your vibration and attract abundance and prosperity** continuously.

Do you Tithe regularly and request your ten-fold return? Remember to **feel good about your tithes**. Feeling fulfilled, expansive and generous when you give allows more to flow back to you.

To be rich, you first have to feel rich. Are you doing something on a regular basis that makes you feel rich?

Are you **getting excited** when things don't go to plan? Feeling like there is something magical on the way when everything goes wrong, allows the creation of something magical!

Are you saying the **Abundance Affirmation and feeling it in every cell of your body, mind and spirit?** Remember to use the arm actions and really feel yourself pulling the Prosperity into your body

Do you truly believe that **the Universe loves you and supports you and wants more for you** than you do for yourself? Are you connecting to that love on a consistent basis? Do you understand that love can flow to you through anything you desire? Feel that love, let it flow through you and embrace it with every cell of your body, mind and spirit. Your life will become effortless and exhilarating when you fully connect with the power of the Universe; that is the power within you!

 Wildly Wealthy Action Tip

Do something every day that moves you towards the Abundance and Prosperity that is waiting for you.

Spirit to Spirit

'Every moment of your life is infinitely creative
and the universe is endlessly bountiful.
Just put forth a clear enough request,
and everything your heart desires must come to you.'

SHAKTI GAWAIN

Namaste — The Divine in me honours and blesses the Divine in you.

It **has been** an honour spending this time with you and sharing my story from financial chaos to Wildly Wealthy Woman! Your journey to prosperity should now be far easier and faster – you have secrets it took me years to discover. By applying these secrets, <u>you too can create the life of your dreams</u>. You have the power within you and now you know how to use that power to create a life of abundance and prosperity.

Mankind is standing on the threshold of a new era and is awakening to the knowledge that **we all have the power to create a joyous, prosperous future**. There has never been a better time in history than right now to discover the truth about who you really are (a divine being) and what you can achieve (absolutely anything your heart desires).

My purpose with this book, my recordings and live mentoring is to support you and give you a much deeper understanding of these Universal Truths.

We are all divine beings living together on this wondrous planet. You may not be able to see your wings, but you do have them. **You are a gift from heaven** and as such, the Universe loves you, adores you and wants only the best for you... including a <u>life filled with continuous and unlimited Prosperity</u>.

Just remember at all times to... **feel Rich, feel Wealthy, feel Abundant and feel Prosperous. Know that <u>your feelings create</u>**

and when you **feel it often enough**, it will come to you – it has to happen, there can be no other outcome, <u>the Universe WILL deliver</u>!

I wish for you Avalanches of Abundance, Mountains of Money, Fabulous Financial Freedom and the happiness and love you deserve. I look forward to hearing how **you too have become Wildly Wealthy**!

Wildly Wealthy Resources

I have given you as much information as I could possibly fit into this book although there is still so much more that will assist you to take a quantum leap into that abundance stream.

If you would like additional guidance and support in applying these principles in your life – or would like to learn even more wonderful ways to become Wildly Wealthy, visit www.WildlyWealthy.com There you will find additional free prosperity articles, information and resources as well as recordings and live international events, including :

◊ Hidden Treasure e-book – over 101 ways to find more money in your life

◊ Tracking Money sheet

◊ Qualities that attract or repel Prosperity

◊ Prosperity Affirmations

◊ Top 10 Secrets to Prosperity

◊ Recommended Reading List for Prosperity

◊ Your own copy of The Abundance Affirmation

◊ 7 Secrets of Millionaires

◊ Monthly Mastermind call

◊ Subliminal CDs

◊ Wildly Wealthy FAST Companion Workbook

◊ Live Teleseminars around the world

And much, much more!

Get Your FREE Resources at
www.WildlyWealthy.com

Notes

My sources for the quotes in this book have been many and varied, including many books and on-line sources as well as those listed below. If you would like my recommended reading list of powerful books that will change the way you think, visit www.WildlyWealthy.com

Abraham - *www.Abraham-Hicks.com*

Allen, James - *As a Man Thinketh*

Beattie, Melody - *Gratitude; Confirming the good things in life*

Ban Breathnach, Sara - *Simple Abundance*

Beecher Stowe, Harriet - *Uncle Tom's Cabin*

Burley, John R. - *Money Secrets of the Rich*

Butterworth, Eric - *Spiritual Economics*

Carlson, Richard - *Don't Worry, Make Money*

Chopra, Deepak - *Keys to Affluence*

Cota-Robles, Patricia D – *It is time for you to be Financially free*

Dore, Carol – *www.caroledore.com*

Dooley, Mike - *Notes from the Universe www.tut.com*

Dyer, Dr. Wayne - *You'll see It When you Believe It*

Einstein, Albert - *Out of My Later Life*

Fieger, Leslie - *The Initiation*

Gawain, Shakti - *Creative Visualization*

Henderson, Robyn - *www.seachangepublishing.com.au*

Hill, Napoleon - *Think and Grow Rich*

Hinton, Candye - *www.thekoach.com*

Mandino, Og - *The Greatest Salesman in the World*

Northrup, Christiane - *Women's Bodies, Women's Wisdom*

Ponder, Catherine - *The Dynamic Laws of Prosperity*

Rohn, Jim - *The Treasury of Quotes*

Scott, Melissa – *www.equinoxlifecoaching.com*

Stanley, Thomas J. and William D. Danko - *The Millionaire Next Door*

Train, John - *The Dance of the Money Bees*

Wattles, Wallace D. - *The Science of Getting Rich*